This is a book about the little people; but it is also a book about elders, the old culture, the Sundance, dreams, the Ponca Tribe of Nebraska, healing, joy, and being Indian. It is the story of Cliff Taylor stumbling into his people's ways and then finding community and home, of him shedding the bindings of trauma and getting his soul back; it is the story of a young Ponca walking with the little people on a journey of cultural recovery/regeneration and remembrance. Part Letter To A Young Native, part Sundancer's memoir, The Memory of Souls is both a back pocket talisman and an old prayer song sung into the night for the future generations.

The Memory of Souls

CLIFF TAYLOR

To Joe Badmoccasin

Thanks for the help

"When I am gone, I don't know what will happen. Maybe one of the boys will have the power and a vision. Maybe they will follow it. But then maybe it will skip them and pass to the next generation. I don't know, but it will continue."

Joe Eagle Elk in The Price of a Gift:
A Lakota Healer's Story

I have a good friend whose grandpa was an Indian doctor. I've listened to this friend tell me stories about his grandpa for the last eleven years, never running out of them, rarely telling the same one twice. When we first met his grandpa, by then deceased, came to me in a dream. I think my friend kind of saw this as his beloved grandpa vouching for me. We've been like brothers ever since.

One of the first stories he told me, maybe even on that first night we met and really dug into it all for about ten hours straight, involved him and his grandpa sitting outside in the backyard up on the reservation he grew up on. He said he and his grandpa were just carrying on, doing normal wasting-away-the-afternoon type stuff, when his grandpa sort of stopped and pointed over to this hill behind him with his face. My buddy said he followed his grandpa's face-point and saw a tiny little

Indian person -one of the little people- standing off a ways up on that hill. His grandpa told him, "They're always watching," and then he resumed their casual joking and afternoon chit chat.

My friend told me this story when we first met because I was telling him about myself, about dreams and visions I'd had, about spirits that came to me, about my own knowledge and interactions, specifically, with the little people. I was twenty three years old and the little people had just started coming to me. They seemed pretty powerful, pretty interesting, pretty wise, humorous, loving and cool -and I was interested in seeing what my friend knew about them. I was just at the beginning of the journey that I hope to somewhat sketch out, share, remember and describe in this little book. I was hungry for knowledge, in general, but also for knowledge of the little people in particular. "My grandpa told me that there are seven different kinds of little people," he said, and then he told me that childhood experience he had with one. I listened closely and filed it away.

This book is for the little people, as a gift of thanks for them and as a gift of Indian love and soul to whoever reads it because of their own interest in or relationship with the little people; it is also, hopefully, a choice selection from that file I've been putting together on them (for various reasons that'll become clear as the story unfolds) for the last eleven years. I hope it adds to the literature in a positive way; I hope it adds to your life in a positive way.

My friend as a kid with his grandpa in the backyard, seeing one of the little people who was standing off in the grass watching the two of them. My friend was not scared. He loved his grandpa. He was learning. "They're always watching," his grandpa said, and then they continued on.

I didn't grow up on a reservation but I did grow up like a lot of Indians today: away from my people's culture, in a household choked with violence, alcohol and abuse, poor, with parents that were about as broken and wounded as it gets.

I grew up in Columbus, a small town in Nebraska, population eighteen thousand or so. There were two Indian families in town, ours and my dad's friend's. I was an art kid, shy, into comic books, horror movies and reading. I experienced a lot of crazy shit and met some amazing friends who saved my life when I was a teenager (I wrote a different book about that, give it a read if you're interested). When I was eighteen I had a vision and then my life became soaked with spirituality and different kinds of spiritual experiences and it has been so ever since. I felt lost, I wandered, I went to college, dropped out, worked at a truck stop for a year, moved away from my hometown, and then, when I was twenty two, I stumbled into the ceremonial world of my people. Like my friend with his grandpa, I started learning some. Slowly, I felt less lost. Slowly, I began to feel better.

I was at this panel discussion a few months ago for this documentary about the under-acknowledged role our women played in the civil-rights work and battles of the American Indian Movement days. The auditorium was full. It was kind of tough to watch the clips the filmmakers had brought, to listen to the stories the Indian grandma and her daughter -who were in the documentary- told. It was like this hand just touching all this still-raw pain I had inside myself. I wanted to get up and leave, just not feel the shit I was feeling in there as so much of our people's tough and tragic, suffering-filled story was recounted. But I stuck it out because, I guess, a guy's supposed to be strong even if he doesn't feel like it or feel like he is; because we've got to be strong for our people; because, you know?

But one thing I noticed was how the two Indian women answered almost every question they were asked with a story. To answer, they told a story. I wondered if anyone else noticed this. The telling of a story includes almost everything that makes us Indian people who we are. All the dimensions of a human being are stimulated and pulled into the act and process when a person is telling a story that really means something to them, that is about things that matter. The same is potentially touched in the listener, or listeners -all those dimensions that make us up, that make us who we are. To tell a story is to be true to the whole of life, our particular conceptualizations about the nature of that whole secondary and unable to substantially interfere with what is actually happening: a person is speaking, the whole mystery of their life and person, of their soul, is speaking, communicating, sharing. What we talk about lives. As long as we tell our stories, we are alive.

There's more to say about stories but I'm thinking about those women because this book is also maybe me telling some stories in response and as answer to a lot of questions that I've thought about, struggled with, that I've been asking my relatives, elders, medicine men, others, the spirits and even these little people sometimes. Maybe some of these questions constitute like a major piece of the inner life that our Indian people almost universally find themselves in strange, sometimes terrible possession of in this day and age. I guess this book is some of the story of how I tried to get to the bottom of some of these big questions that modern Indian people are afflicted with. Hopefully some of

these stories will answer or at the very least pro-
vide some serious food for thought when it comes
to these questions. That is the hope.

The questions: What does it mean to be Indian, especially in America today? Why try? Where
does all this pain come from? What about our ancestors, how can we honor them? How can we help
our loved ones, our relatives, our communities, our
tribes, ourselves? What the fuck's up with all the
drugs and alcohol? Can we be healed, and how?
What about the past? What about the future? How
can I learn about my people, our culture, myself as
an Indian? What're we supposed to do? What do
the old ones have to say? What should I be asking?
How do we start?

When I was twenty two I met this medicine
man named Joe Badmoccasin. He told a story
about when he first met his primary teacher, Joe
Eagle Elk. Joe at that point was an Episcopalian
minister with a master's degree in sociology. He
said he saw so many things happen in Joe Eagle
Elk's ceremonies, was rocked by how much this
humble man knew and just had a million questions
he wanted to ask him. He said one day this began to come up and Joe Eagle Elk told him, "Just
watch. Listen. Observe."

When I was young and hanging around
Joe Bad I was kind of the same way. I wanted all
sorts of knowledge and truths and information and

ANSWERS to all my QUESTIONS. But instead I got very little of that, directly, at least; instead I heard stories, experienced things, just absorbed all sorts of things day by day in the course of living, sweating, helping out and mainly just being some small character in the background. Weirdly, what I found as I reflected on it all years later, was that the questions I had never really got answered all that much but the thing inside of me asking all the questions sort of did get slaked, soothed, stilled, grown some, and educated. From Joe Bad I learned that it's not so much about getting all the questions in our mind answered as it is about getting our spirit into learning what it needs to so that we can become who we're supposed to and have some peace.

In this book I'm going to write about the little people some (to honor them), tell some stories, try to answer some of those questions, and share some of the things I've learned with my spirit. I guess we'll see how it goes.

As my one friend says, "Well, let's do it then."

In my early twenties I was introduced to the sweats and to the spirituality of my people. It was like love at first sight. I'd never sweat before and then I was sweating once or twice a week for two years straight.

Going to the sweat I met all sorts of people. Growing up, I don't think I ever heard an Indian relative of mine talk to me about anything spiritual, really, but once I started sweating I was treated to an almost unimaginable superabundance of Indians talking about spiritual things. There were elders, medicine men, Sundancers, pipe-carriers, heyo-kas, dreamers, psychically-gifted people, prayerful people and spiritual people of all kinds. I listened as a shy young man as life stories, dreams, visions, incidents of healing, and powerful memories of every sort were generously shared. It was like being washed by the sacred spirit-waters of the ancestors. New rooms grew inside of me to accommodate what was being passed around, to accommodate new aspects of my spiritual life that were waking up within me. I met Leonard Crow Dog. Spirits began coming to me in dreams. It was transforming. It was unbelievable.

Within the first couple months of my going to the sweat all the time I met an interesting, outspoken, very intelligent and salty old Lakota woman. I bumped into her at the University and we got to chatting, she said she was finally finishing up her degree. The next time I bumped into her, a few weeks later, she said, "I had a vision of you." I sat down. "Oh yeah?" (I think this was the first time anyone ever had a vision of me, that I'm aware of at least.)

"I was sitting at my kitchen table," she said, "looking out my back window and then there you were, standing there by my garden, looking in at me."

"Wow."

"I think I'm supposed to do a divination for you."

"A what?"

We sat there and she began to tell me her life story. She was in her fifties, the daughter of a well-known local medicine man whom she was estranged from. She'd had experiences and had seen things since she was a little girl, explored all sorts of spiritual paths over the years, was writing and researching a book, and had recently returned from Africa after completing a three year training with a Dagara medicine man named Malidoma Some. She said she worked with these spirits called the little people and did a form of divination the Dagara people referred to as 'stick divining.' She had a hardy presence, a rich vocabulary. When she asked me if I'd be interested I very open-mindedly told her sure. We arranged a time and day for the divination, she wrote me down her address and then she told me, "You need to bring them a question and also a coin." I thought about what she'd said and then I said, "Okay."

We had the divination the following week in her dusty, cluttered garage. The night before I had a dream where she and I were walking the aisles of a liquor store. We found a particular brand of vodka. She grabbed a small bottle of it and said, "Bring this as an offering for the little people too." When I woke up I went down to the liquor store and bought the vodka from my dream. When I showed up with it and told her about the dream she laughed and thought it was pretty funny. "The little people enjoy a little alcohol every now and then. Over in Africa we drank a beer that the little people had taught the Dagara how to make. It wasn't that good. It was kind of weak."

This woman prayed aloud in front of an altar she had set up on an old chest-of-drawers, shaking her rattles, calling on her ancestors, on the plants and animals and waters, on mountains and thunderclouds, on these little people friends of hers. After that part of the divination we sat down with this homemade symbol-laden mat between us. She had a stick that would've made a good play-gun when you were a kid. She sat bent over, listening, her eyes closed, something else moving her hand around. I respectfully watched and listened (I could feel a lighter version of the vibrations that accompanied the presence of the spirits in the ceremonies the medicine men did).

She told me a number of things, each of

which branch out into their own story that will not be shared here for various practical reasons, but the main thing that she said was this: "You have little people. They walk with you. And they want you to call them."

The divination lasted about twenty minutes. When it was over we went inside to her kitchen table and talked about it.

"So, what does that mean? That I have little people and I'm supposed to call them?"

"It means exactly that: they want you to call them."

I was very nervous. As far as I was concerned or knew, only medicine men called the spirits. I respected the ways too much to play around or behave like I was something special, doing shit I didn't really know anything about.

"I don't know if I'm comfortable doing that."

She was insistent, pushy almost. "It's like they told you they want to start talking to you on the phone every once in awhile. If you don't pick up the phone and call them how are you going to have a conversation with them? Calling them is like picking up the phone and dialing their number."

"Oh," I said, uncertain-feeling. "Okay."

After about two hours of kitchen table talk I went home. I didn't doubt anything about this lady

or her divination but I just wasn't really comfortable with the instructions I'd received. But also, at
the time, I'd heard more than one older person say,
"You're supposed to do what the spirits tell you."
Back then I was in full learning mode and trying
my best to listen to the things I was hearing from
all these spiritual relatives of mine. I felt kind of
conflicted, a little afraid of messing up. I decided
I'd make an offering and pray.

In my apartment, in the afternoon with all
the downtown traffic noisy outside my window, I
got a bowl, a little food, some water, some tobacco
and some sage. I lit the sage and set it down with
the bowl of offerings on the floor in my bedroom
and prayed.

"In my heart, I believe," I prayed to these
little people, "but if you really want me to do these
things, to call you, then you're going to have to
give me an experience, so that my mind can believe too."

I prayed and then, needing to get some sleep
before I went to my thirdshift job at the grocery
store, I crashed out.

That evening I had a powerful dream with
one of these little people in it.

I dreamed of a little old man, maybe two to

two and a half feet tall. The dream is too special
for me to share here but I will say that he gave me
some things, shared with me his name and told me,
"Call me and I will come to help you." He also
talked to me some about a kind of assignment we
were to work on. "We need to fix the memory of
souls," he said. I repeated this back to him, "We
need to fix the memory of souls...to heal the people." "Yes," he said, "to heal the people."

When I woke up from this dream it was like
a strange, sacred music box had been clicked open
deep inside me and it began to play for a long,
long time -and maybe it is sort of still playing right
now even. The dream had a strong, intimate after-
glow. I prayed and received an immediate answer.
The things shown to me in the dream were sacred,
mysterious, wet with blessings in a way that would
never change; permanently so. I sat in my bed and
hummed with a nighttime kind of awe, cut and quiet. The dream crackled inside me like a small fire.

I wound up taking this dream to several
medicine men and pipe-carriers over the years.
It was a big dream and I desired to understand it,
to have it interpreted for me. Oddly, it seemed to
resist deciphering. The Lakota woman who did
the divination for me seemed almost caught off
guard by its depth of content, excited, genuinely
puzzled. I told it during a house-ceremony a Rosebud medicine man did and he said he'd share with

me his understanding after the ceremony; later, he
shared what seemed like a bunch of unrelated BS
to me. At the time I palled around quite a bit with
this older Native potter and artist who was just
returning to the culture after doing some time and
he said, "You need to tell your Wichasa Wakan Joe
that dream." I nodded and said okay. It was weird
but even though I was a close part of Joe's circle
for two years -Sundancing with him, going to his
ceremonies, helping him out with stuff -I was very
shy about bringing up the different experiences
and dreams I had. I had a tremendous respect for
Joe. His stories were like manna to me, like food
raining down slowly from a luminous starlit heav-
en. I'd read so many books about seekers meeting
and then learning from spiritual teachers of great
wisdom and power. Being a part of Joe's circle
for the two years that I was was the one and only
time in my life where I finally found myself in a
semi-real version of this storybook fantasy reality.
I was such a kid and in so many ways, he was such
the real deal. Maybe I didn't want to appear like I
was some dingbat vying for extra attention because
I was some extra special guy. Maybe I was des-
perate to show my trueness and tried to do so with
my quietness, my good kid-ness, my not asking for
anything extra. Whatever the case, I rarely brought
up my experiences and stuff to Joe; but I did bring
up this dream eventually, nearly a year after I had

it, at my second Sundance. I planned to tell this
story later but I guess we'll tell it now.

After I had the dream I began to call this
little old man and his other relatives in the sweat
regularly. It was hard. I'd call them and then I'd
feel this energy -a lot of times but not every time-
fill my body. It was so overwhelming, so sacred, so
holy, so emotional, so powerful. It was like deep
inside the human heart there was this spot where
all the different kinds of tears a person could cry
met and shared a single common grief-filled nature and their coming into the lodge would touch
that spot and I'd start crying, loudly and almost
uncontrollably. I felt the bottomless suffering of
the world, the ineffable beauty of life, the immea-
surable, infinite power of the Other World. I was
taken into the intricacies of so many souls that
were struggling to make their way in this world.
I was a glass overflowing with the water of the
spirits, a glass packed full of the sand of higher
materials. My capacity for feeling was tore open
and afterwards when I was left to heal up, that
capacity would knit itself back together as bigger,
able to contain more, able to handle and withstand
more. Among all these tough relatives of mine,
scarred up, having seen a lot of the dark side of
life, I would cry out embarrassingly like a young
wounded animal. Those little people would come
and their energy was so holy and intense that it just

made me cry for all the things I saw and felt in that expanded state. It was good, like a bloodletting giving me my soul and its abilities back, but it was hard; honest like a prehistoric thunderstorm; real like the worst kinds of pain; holy like love.

This happened for maybe a year or a year and a half. It happened during a purification sweat at our Sundance. And that time, teary and vulnerable-feeling, I did tell Joe my dream.

His little diabetes-sapped body sat on a chair by the sweat fire and I sat on the ground telling him the dream. Night fell on the grounds, the fire whipped and burned. I was scared, not knowing what was happening, fearful of the dream's bigness. Joe's reaction was not like I expected; he was not lost to seriousness but more he had a grandfather's excitement, fear-dispelling sense of humor about it almost. He listened and then he said, "Tomorrow we're going to have a ceremony." He laughed some, like this was the fun part. "During the ceremony I'm going to have you sit in the middle, Cliff. The spirits'll doctor you. It's time for you to be crucified."

He laughed at that, rubbed his hands together.

"They're gonna crucify you."

The next night we had a ceremony in the basement of one of our Sundance leaders (decades earlier the same basement had been used for cer-

emonies by another medicine man since passed).
Joe set up his altar in the middle of the asymmet-
rical space. My little brother sat beside me. When
the lights were turned off and the songs sung the
spirits came in and Joe's rattles lifted up and took
off. They flew all around, spewing sparks, shaking at a perfect, inhuman speed. Joe listened and
relayed what the spirits had to say. "Cliff," he
said, "they said you and your brother need to learn
to depend on one another, to lean on each other,
because as your life goes on you two will be all of
the family that you have." The basement was thick
with invisible presences. It was crowded like a
street in New York. I hung my head, kept my eyes
closed and prayed.

About midway through the ceremony Joe
had me come over the tobacco ties and into his
altar. He covered me with a blanket and then the
rattles really went to work on me, leaping, circling
and battering me, brushing and doctoring me. I
instantly began crying for all the energies and
power of it. I was like a hole made with the fingers of a hand opened up into a hole the size of my
whole body and this tsunami of energy was roaring
through me. I became a portal for this huge flood
of tears to come through, the tears of countless
people, of countless parties, and I bawled them all,
bellowed and sobbed, felt my whole body pouring
out all these tears, all this emotion, all this other-

worldly energy, a whole world of tears. This went on and on and then the rattles left, indicating that the spirits were done. I folded back down to something that resembled normal, spent, hollowed almost, but somewhat normal. "They're done now," Joe told me quietly, using his hands to direct me that I should then go back to my seat.

After that ceremony we all ate menudo and frybread upstairs, Eddie and the Cruisers playing on the big screen in the living room. We all carried on like usual, laughing and making conversation. In the kitchen, Joe said, "There were a lot of other spirits down there, Cliff, ones I didn't know. It was a packed house." That was his total post-ceremony commentary. I thought about it for a second and then just politely kept eating and listening to Joe talk about other things.

Joe never interpreted my dream and he never brought it up again either; but he did do that ceremony for me and I don't know exactly what happened during it but I've always been sure that it was something that helped.

Within a week of that divination and dream I had another dream.

In this one I was in a house encountering this frightening, monstrously large version of my

father. It seemed like more than some normal psy-
chological dream to me; it was scarier. For whatever reason, I began to call that little old man, my
spirit-helper, and his relatives the other little people. I prayed and called them in the dream and then
in a blink I was in a different dream.

Now I was small and looking up, like a baby
looking up out of a crib; and surrounding me in
a loving half-circle were about five of these little
people -but slightly different looking. They were
also just a couple feet tall but instead of minia-
ture-looking humans they were almost like angelic
gremlins. They were naked, luminously green-
skinned, pointy-eared and completely smooth and
without genitals in their crotch areas. This be-
yond-human utterly trust-inspiring warming love
sweetness radiated out of them, like this sweetness
was their true nature, and it cut me right to my
core. I breathed this love of theirs in with all of my
pores. I looked at them closely to take in their fea-
tures and appearance. Then, telepathically, I asked
them, "Which one of you is --------?"

I scanned them and then this one at the end
almost shyly looked down and to the ground; it
was him, he was my helper, the little old man in
another of his forms. I kind of met him in kind
and looked over these little beings, studying them
in the lucidity of the dream, all the while really
checking out my friend out of the corner of my

eye, indirectly, gently. I looked them over, felt their special love and sweetness, and then woke up.

This dream, my second of the little people in a week, was more in what became a long, slow process of them introducing themselves to me, of us building up our relations, of me gathering an understanding of them.

This dream is significant because I've always felt like that indescribable love-sweetness of theirs I experienced is like their signature, the essential feeling-print (like an identifying fingerprint or track) of their kind's spirit. In this dream I was given a taste of their true essence, almost like so I could find them and know them and remember them properly; also maybe so my growing knowledge of them could begin on the right sort of solid, basic foundation. The word is sweetness, like the no-strings-attached kind of affection given to you by someone who truly loves you, but I have a hard time finding the perfect same-sweetness-generating analog. It was a sweetness like the smell of night on the wind during a perfect hour in the wilderness. It was sweetness like the kind that just makes you want to close your eyes and smile softly. It was sweetness like many different kinds of love all wrapped up into one.

This second dream was like many things the little people would give to me over the years: a gift I still find myself occasionally handling and thinking about today.

Indians have lived in a close, reverential relationship with Nature and the spirit-dimensions for thousands and thousands of years. In short, this way of living has gelled into a different kind of consciousness and culture and being. The wisdom and ways of our ancestors are coded into our spirit, our DNA; and although this lifeway of ours has been disrupted immensely in the past hundred years and then some, the roots of our consciousness and culture run much deeper than the West can conceptualize, much deeper than their campaign of decimation has so far been able to reach.

We Indian people are made of rich, resilient stuff. Thousands and thousands of years of the most pure and self-sacrificing human prayers possible protect us and continue to carry us forward. We are of the land and as such, will ultimately outlast the unsustainable monsters of modernity. We're older than this out-of-control story that so many think is the only story. We have a staying-power crafted by all the creatures and critters of the earth, by our Mother the planet herself, by the stars and our relatives in the greater cosmos, and by the Great Spirit, the Maker of life itself. We carry things, sacred things. We have something to say, to contribute. We Indians are this ancient land, speaking, singing, praying, and being. Like our relatives the little people, we were here before this party and we'll be here after it's over; we aren't going anywhere.

So who are the little people?

When Joe Bad's teacher Joe Eagle Elk was a young man working as a farm hand in Western Nebraska he started seeing one of these little people every once in awhile, peeking at him in the stable, watching him as he got up in the early hours to go and milk the cows. It threw him off a little, seeing this tiny little Indian person here and there as he was trying to go about his business and do his work. Eventually he went to ask his uncle about it. Ceremonies were done and then he went up on the hill to fast. When he was up on the hill two of these little people came to him and told him that they were going to be his friends. They told him their names, gave him songs to sing for when he called them, and gave him instructions for how to set up his altar. They told him that during his ceremonies they would come and use the knowledge and powers of their kind to help him and his people. After he came down from the hill he did as they instructed him to, working closely with these two little people friends of his, and a vast amount of help and good and healing(s) and blessings came to his friends and relatives. This was how Joe

Eagle Elk began his career as a medicine man.

Our people have lived in a culture that very carefully and knowingly stimulates and nurtures spirit-awareness. Life is more than just what our physical eyes can see; that 'more' is seen into with the eye of the heart, the eye of the spirit; this spirit-awareness. This expanded awareness unveils the reality of the spirit-world. Through experiences and conversations, had in dreams, visions, and ceremonies, we came to know our spirit relatives, with whom our lives are interwoven. For as long as we can remember this dimension of life, the spirit-world, has been integrated into the very heart of our culture and everyday life.

There are many Nations of spirits and the little people are one of them. When I asked my Sundance Chief in Santee about them he said, "We call them the Chahochina; which means: 'they live in the trees' or 'the boys who live in the woods.' Everything that we've lost, they still have. Everything that we once possessed but appear to have lost, they still possess and have knowledge of. They are what we should be. They live how we used to live. They're playful, they're loving, they're wise, they're sacred."

The little people, like many of our relatives in the spirit-world that we have relations with dating back untold millennia, have and maintain hope that us people can right and correct our course, returning back to a life that revolves around the sacred, honors and protects and loves the land and the animals, the plants and the water, that doesn't move towards destruction but creation and renewal, spirituality and love. The little people have been working with our Indian people for as long as we can remember. They're our relatives in this big, beautiful earth family that we're a part of. They continue to come to us today, despite the amnesia that pervades the people and the times. Like they came to Joe Eagle Elk, making him into an Indian doctor for his people. Like they came to me, becoming my friends as I went on my own journey of healing and remembering as just a regular, lost Ponca guy.

And the little people are everywhere too. They, like us humans, are worldwide; and they've been chummy friends to all sorts of people from all sorts of cultures and civilizations. Everyone knows about them as being the Leprechauns to the Irish. The Hawaiians have their own long-standing knowledge, name for, and relations with them. Same goes for countless peoples everywhere, especially among the Indigenous. I met a four hundred pound legless Aboriginal spirit-healer from Australia once and we talked about the little people. The night before our talk he said a few of our Indian little people had come into his tent to check him out. He said that when he was a little boy his mom would set out food for them in their kitchen and sometimes they'd show up to come and get it. "Back when all the continents were one," he told me, "during the time of Pangea, the little people were at the top of the food chain." Who knows?

I've had little people come to me from India, Africa, Ireland, Nebraska. They're spirit-beings. They live in Nature, in the interiors of the non-animal life-forms that make up the natural world; hence their vast knowledge of the deep layers of earth life. They're just like us, with their own culture, language, and spirituality, varying slightly in looks and ways according to climate and place. Like many mysteries in life, there's more to them than we'll probably ever know; but maybe the most important unifying piece of knowledge about them that we do know, and which is shared by many around the world, is this: they are our relatives and they want to help.

Thinking of little people stories, this one comes to mind-

Maybe about five years ago I found myself deep in a late fall funk. It'd been an all right year but this seemed to regularly be my season for depression, despair, sadness over what I felt was missing, was lacking from my life. It was my night

off and I just felt like a broken, shit-covered ant
stuck in a thousand room maze where every room
was full of mortal loneliness. This work of helping
the people is so fucking lonely, I thought to myself; And it never seems to change.

Well, I hadn't had a drink in maybe a year
but on this particular night I was just so hungry for
some companionship and normalcy, the comforts
of just being around people my age doing stuff a
lot of them did: drinking, hanging out at the bar,
bullshitting, searching in the back of their minds
for someone to be with. I tried and mostly succeed-
ed in not drinking for spiritual reasons for about
nine years. This wound up being one of those
nights where my commitment and resolve crum-
bled. I felt bad in so many ways. I lit some sage,
apologized to all the different spirits who came to
me regularly, told them that I was dying of loneliness, was going downtown to have a drink, and
then put on my coat and went downtown.

I went to my bar, O'Rourke's, a work-
ing-class/young art people's gritty and worn
down bar. One time, drinking there on a snowy
afternoon, all of us in the smoker's garden were
witness to this gorgeous falcon's landing and then
hanging out in the sidewalk tree in front of us. It
was a magnificent creature anomalously appearing in the heart of the city. We drank and checked
it out, laughed and speculated about it. Howev-

er we all saw it, almost across the board, for the
hour it stayed in that tree, we all felt VISITED.
O'Rourke's could occasionally be a pretty magical
place.

I found a stool at the bar and ordered myself
a cheap draw. The atmosphere of the place immediately began working on me. It's hard always being different, always feeling different, even if it's
for some pretty good, even sacred reasons. O'Rourke's was always quick to give me this feeling of
being welcomed in to the world of everybody else.
Probably the possibility of getting to have what
everybody else had came with this too. It was a
kind of toasty relief, relaxation, release. My bad
feelings disappeared into the background. The beer
warmed and blessed me from the inside.

About three quarters of the way through that
first beer, as I was sorting through all these feelings, the little people showed up. I saw about six
or seven of them playing around and running along
the bar. They were like some goofy theater troupe,
somersaulting and dancing around all the beer bottles and glasses, hopping over people's hands and
arms. Their sight and antics brought a smile out of
my mellowing sadness. "We love you this much,"
they said. "We are here with you even now." They
talked to me for a few minutes and then they left
and I kept drinking.

That night the little people talked to me like

older brothers who understood what was going on with me -they were encouraging, kind, support-ive; they talked to me about my life, my destiny, spiritual things, letting me know that they would always be there for me no matter what, whether I was up or down, whether I was strong and on point, or weak feeling and skidding out; and then, once they'd patted that message and reassurance into my spirit, they took off and let me return back to my drinking, to the tending of my needs.

And that night I did drink, drinking till close and getting good and drunk. Their visit to me at my bar when I felt so fucking low was like a par-ticular kind of poem about their almost realistic and yet unconditional compassion they had for me, their twenty-something human friend and relative. The book of poetry my heart was writing about them probably needed that poem of their popping in to see me at the bar when I was depressed and just wanted to get fucked up. I learned again of the strength of our relationship, how much my help-ers were really there for me. But it was real, too. I wasn't scolded or reprimanded or anything. I was allowed to just be human, just be myself. I drank that night for hours and hours after they left and felt no regret. My spirituality and my humanity blurred together. It was sad, sweet, real, Indian, modern, hard, beautiful, and necessary.

And that wasn't the only night they came to

O'Rourke's over the years. There were other nights like that too. I remember a series of them where, about two beers in, they'd come and talk with me while I smoked by myself out in the smoker's garden. I'd smoke, look out onto the cold downtown scene, and listen to them talk to me about spiritual things. I felt so Indian. Drinking and alone in a culture where my people were little more than an unremembered footnote to most, listening to the spirits, these true caretakers of the land and life of America, talk to me about the deeper reality, learning from them like my ancestors did, but as real and regular and half-lost as the other guy drinking by himself and staring off into space at the table a few feet away from me. These little people would fill me with strings of understandings as I smoked and then they'd take off and let me drink the rest of my night away. To me, this was real spirituality. It came to you even at the bar. It found you when you needed it most. It made you feel complex, real, contradictory, soulful and extra-alive.

One time while smoking outside the gas station where I work, they came and, among other things, said, "We are not just *your* relatives but you are *our* relative. We are not just *your* family but you are *our* family. Do you understand?"

I talked back to them in my mind.

Yes, I did.

One of the coolest parts of traveling around Indian Country and going to sweats and Sundances was hearing all the priceless, stored-in-the-heart stories people had to share. Despite being a voracious reader I read very few Indian books. I wanted to learn about my people directly from my people, not from what was inside books but from what was inside them, in their words, their spirits, their eyes, the immense presence -like those Cottonwoods at the Sundance grounds that were hundreds of years old- of their lives. One part of my being was like a collector, never writing anything down, but very conscientious of the value of what was being shared, told, spoken, relayed; I let it all seep into me, spontaneously file itself away into my memory. All our ancestors had was their memory so I figured however my memory worked in capturing all this sacred material would be good enough for me too. I would put my faith in what they did. I would be like them and that would be good enough for me.

Stories of all kinds filtered into the glowing recesses of my memory; all the things my relatives talked about in ceremony, around the campfire, at the kitchen table, while working, on road trips, gathered and amassed within me. It felt good to be full of the talk and understandings of my people,

like I had a medicine bundle of pure Indian soul
packed away inside my spirit. I chewed on and
sorted through these stories, contemplated them,
felt the specific mysteries of them. Maybe this
was one of the things being Indian meant: to be
deeply full in your heart and soul of all the things
your relatives talk about and share, and to be oc-
cupied with thinking about it all. I loved it. Every
story was a jewel, a polished river stone. One time
a friend told me, "You start out with nothing but
then each story you hear is like a pebble. You take
the pebble and toss it behind you. Throughout the
course of just living these pebbles -about all sorts
of things- keep coming to you, you keep tossing
them over your shoulder behind you, and then
one day you see that you've accumulated a small
mountain of these pebbles. Now, when someone
asks you about something, you maybe have a pebble or a few about it -before you had nothing but
now you find yourself having something to contribute. All these stories are like pebbles; just keep
collecting them; just keep tossing them onto the
pile behind you."

    This friend of mine is pretty wise. He also
told me, "Pay attention to the details of these stories, to the words people use, the pauses; because
there's a lot of important information packed into
those things."

    I collected pebbles about a lot of things;

less often as an active questioner, usually just as
a listener, another young guy just quietly taking
in the story that was being told. People talked
about their youth and growing up, their missteps,
their relationships, jobs, what you'd expect, but
they also talked about their dreams, medicine men
they'd known, Sundancing, sacred things, super-
natural encounters, Bigfoot, medicine conflicts,
ghosts, the lives of a multitude of sacred objects,
from spherical stones to mummified hands, star
knowledge, the appearance of humans in previous
Ages, ceremonial burial practices for the corpses
of giants, and on and on; I listened in fascination
and a sort of restrained wonder to it all, feeling it
penetrating into my being, hoping I'd somehow remember it all even though I knew that I wouldn't.
This kind of story-sharing and storytelling about
sacred things is one of the great treasures and
infinitely powerful core pieces of our Indian people's still-magnificent being and culture. One time
in ceremony Crazy Horse came in and clamped his
enormous hand over my friend's face. My friend
said the hand was wet. The medicine man said,
"That wetness is the blood of the people." All these
stories we hear our relatives tell are wet with the
blood of the people, sacred and important beyond
our knowing.

And of course, once those little people started coming to me I began to collect the pebbles of

their stories as well.

I had an uncle here in Lincoln who was struck by lightning. He was partying at his mom's place and their tiny house was packed. It started thundering and he went to close all the windows, weaving his way around all the drunk and stoned people crammed in there. In the kitchen one of the windows was held open by this steel bar. He grabbed it, stuck his arm with it out the window into the pouring rain and yelled to everyone, "Look! I'm a lightning rod!" And the second he did that he was struck by lightning and shot across the room. "I told Warfield," he said, "and Warfield said, 'you were kissed by the Thunderbird.'"

After he was struck by lightning he was kind of changed; he started seeing things and operating a little differently. Some thought he was a nut, a flake (he gave me a water-damaged copy of The Celestine Prophecy from out of the trunk of his car to read), but I thought he was interesting, a bit wild but legit. And he had a lot of stories to tell.

Without my ever bringing up the little people he began talking to me about them one time while we were drinking coffee in his tannery (a business that failed fairly quickly). He said that when he lived out of town without any electricity they'd come into his house and just hop up onto chairs at his kitchen table and smile and look at him. He said that they had an underground village in our tribe's buffalo pasture and that one time when this was brought up this one guy just laughed his head off, which turned into a dare to go up there by himself for a night, which he did, and then he saw something up there that night that literally turned his hair white and so that was that. But the story of his I liked the most was about my uncle Sandy, then employed as our tribe's historian.

He said he was working the register at my great aunt's Native arts and crafts store in Niobrara when Sandy came in. He said that trailing right behind Sandy, unseen to him, was one of these little people. "What was that all about?" I asked. "That little old man was your uncle Sandy's guardian," he said. "Your uncle Sandy has battled a lot of white man's illnesses the past couple years and that little person is walking with him to help make sure that he accomplishes everything he's here to do before he passes."

Maybe that seems like a small story -and that was the whole of it- but it was big to me because it suggested a Taylor family connection to these little people who'd started coming to me. There they were with my uncle Sandy and here they were with me. These sacred little beings. These spirits. The spirits.

I filed away every story I heard about the little people as I traveled. I just about never brought them up but among Indians, among my relatives,

they came up. Every story about them took me
a little closer to their mystery and spirit, to their
medicine. It was like a stairway into their essence
and my people's essence, and every story grew a
new stair on that stairway, engulfing me further,
showing me more. Like I was always going deeper while also, paradoxically, always already being
fully THERE-

As this little book goes along I will share
some more stories from my little people files. This
book is a poem of praise for them and a humble
storytelling to honor all the genius storytellers I
have been lucky enough to hear and listen to.

Like the kid in the backseat said to me one
night when some shit fell off the truck on our way
to a ceremony-

"Next!"

I danced two years up in Crow Creek with
Joe Bad and then due to some unexpected twists
and turns of fate, I found myself searching out a
new place to finish up my four year commitment.

I checked out Crow Dog's Sundance and
then a newly started one just outside of Lincoln. I
was sort of in a bad way. I needed to finish my four
years but I was also fatigued, lost, overwhelmed,
somewhere between halfways being a new animal

because of our people's ancient, high-end ('the good stuff') spirituality and an exhausted man craving a return to the pedestrian life of fucking around, going to parties, trying to find love, consuming movies and entertainment, and just being young. I quit my job stocking shelves overnights at the grocery store, which I'd been doing for four years, and decided to try to figure some of my shit out. The plan that came to me? Camp out at the Ponca powwow grounds for a week (it was the middle of summer), give a week of my life to my ancestors, and see what happened. If that didn't work then I didn't know what I was going to do.

I set my tent up by the fence line of our tribe's buffalo pasture and mostly just hung out by myself. In the evenings I'd go into the pasture and just walk around for a couple hours, watch the buffalo for awhile, walk past our cemetery, look for stones, and pray. One evening I sat down on the hard earth and prayed and called the little people. I told them that if they didn't help me to find someplace to dance then I was just going to head back to Lincoln, put away all my sacred stuff, and just drink and be a regular person like everyone else for a couple years. I'm not sure if it was wise to give them and my ancestors an ultimatum like that but I was pretty down-and-out feeling, ready to kick all my shit into a river and put it all behind me for awhile (that year the little people talked to me for the first time while awake; they told me when Joe Bad was going to pass). Still shredded and covered in hundreds of wounds from a hellish childhood, I was tore up inside. My family wasn't into the culture. Maybe I was tired of feeling so profoundly different from everyone else. I don't know. I prayed while sitting down on that indescribably beautiful land of my Ponca people and basically said, "Help me or fuck this."

What happened that summer is its own book's worth of characters and stories, dreams and adventures, but needless to say, my prayers were heard and answered in ways I'm still reaping the benefits of, still feeling the blessings of. I went to three Sundances on Santee, the reservation a couple miles over from our powwow grounds. I hit up two powwows. I met boatloads of spiritual people, relatives, people who knew my incarcerated father when he was young. I probably had the most alone time I've ever had in my life. I went up on the hill for the first time. It was a summer that gave me more than any other summer of my life. After I write this little book about the little people I hope to write my next book all about that summer. That's the plan anyway. But I did find the place where I would end up completing my four year commitment and then continue dancing for three more summers after that just because I was still feeling it so strongly. It was the second dance I went to, after my week up at the powwow grounds began its mutation into what would eventually become two months, and it was called Hidden Valley.

Hidden Valley is about five miles off the main road that cuts through Santee. There's a tattered red flag hanging from a Stop sign at the turn off. Four miles of meandering gravel and then a mile of somewhat precarious road through a farmer's field until you come to the secluded Sundance grounds -called Hidden Valley because it's enclosed/cupped in a valley wrapped tight by rolling hills on one side and some thick old woods on the other. There's a freshwater spring there. Half a century ago there was a house there and some relatives lived there; but now that's all gone and there's no trace of the house or anything. This first summer I was there I sat beside an old grandma who seemed to take a liking to me (I knew no one there; I was invited by a fire keeper who met me when I was keeping fire at another Sundance; "Do you see that old man over there?" he asked during the dance, pointing to a spirit with his face; "No," I said.) and she told me that a long time ago, when ceremonies were outlawed and pushed underground they did Sundances there in this valley in secret. "My mom would bring me when I was a little girl," she said. "To keep quiet, instead of using a drum, they used a piece of rawhide and drummed on that. We had people watching for anyone who was coming, to warn us."

I was shy to the point of being almost total-
ly, awkwardly mute but I had a way I'd learned to
get by: I always volunteered to work hard doing
whatever. I threw in with the young guys, was
left behind in their fast-as-light group teasing and
talking (this was a family Sundance; they'd all
known each other since before they could speak),
and just followed along and worked up a sweat
and listened and ate like a pure, well-intentioned
worker. Joe Bad had done his first sweat with the
leaders of this dance when they were young men
a year before I was born in 1980. He was an Episcopalian minister back then, serving congregations
on both sides of the river in Yankton and Santee.
This Sundance was the first of the modern era on
the Santee reservation, started in the mid-eighties
at the request of a mother with fourteen kids who
wanted for there to be a place on her reservation
for her kids and other relations to dance at, instead
of them always having to go somewhere else. Her
cousin Grandpa Earl Swift Hawk, a Rosebud medicine man, came down and built and ran it until he
passed away in his 90s in the late 90s. The summer
I came there it was being run by one of her grand-
sons.

This Sundance was wealthy with history and
I listened like my whole body was just an ear as
everyone bullshitted and caught the young ones up

to speed and talked about loved ones and old times that they loved to talk about. I listened especially closely about how they said the little people lived in the trackless woods across the creek bordering the west side of the grounds. I'd never heard (and nor have I heard at any other place since) so much open talk about the little people before. Everyone there spoke casually about them, laughing, in tones of mystery, awe, puzzlement, reverence, loving humor. I sat beside a one-lunged veteran and his ten year old son, whom he'd brought to the Sundance that year to help him maybe get some healing as the year previous the boy's sister, one of the man's other children, was killed in the Columbine-style school shooting up at Red Lake. The boy finished his pop and set it down in the grass beside his empty chip bag. "Now make sure to pick up after yourself," his dad said. "This land isn't ours. It belongs to the little people. They're just letting us use it."

"Who're the little people?" the boy asked.

"They're spirits, tiny little Indian people who live in those woods over there. And they're real powerful too. The ones who work with them become real powerful medicine men."

Maybe I should've asked him to say some more about them but that wasn't my way. My mind clamped onto what was said like a bear trap but I didn't say a word. I was hungry for knowledge of the little people -they were my helpers after all, I guess- but my shyness, until the very end of the dance, when it was all over and I got to talk with the Sundance Chief one-on-one for awhile, prevented me from being anything more than a listener. This was okay though, because this particular summer the little people were very active and there was plenty for me to soak up.

One of my favorite stories about the little people comes from this first summer at Hidden Valley. It was during the purification days and maybe four of us were up by the fire talking about whatever in the wee hours of the night (this phrase comes from the Irish where they call the little people the 'wee people', I believe, and the 'wee hours' refer to these hours when night is beginning to transition into morning, a time when many have had run-ins with the little people). I was in a kind of storyteller's heaven by that fire, as some of the best stories people have to tell a lot of times tend to come out around that Sundance fire. We were surrounded by quiet, the audibly running creek was just a few yards of rocky bank away, the trees where so much otherworldly activity happened stared back at us with a charge that never seemed to wane. "When we talk about sacred things the spirits say we're 'making medicine'," my Sundance Chief would later tell me. "It's a good thing. It's one of the ways we help each other."

But so we were sitting around the fire on our

cheapo chairs when this ten year old Omaha singer came running up on us, along with the Red Lake kid, out of the darkness. He had a spooked look on his face and was breathing hard. The oldest guy asked him, "What's going on?" The kid paused for a second, probably considering how we were going to react to what he was about to say, and then he said, "We saw the little green men." (A few up there on Santee referred to the little people as the little green men; even Joe Bad did once back at his church in Lincoln. Later, talking with this kid, he would tell me a story about his mom's car breaking down on that farmer's field road one night while coming to Sundance. He said his mom told him and his two siblings that they'd just sleep in the car and then get help with it in the morning. He said that while crashed out in the back seat he was awoken by a tapping on his door's window. He sat up and saw two little green men tapping on the window with their fingers. "Psst, psst. Hey kid, let us in. Psst, psst. You want some candy? Huh? You want some candy? Open the door and let us in." The way he described these little green men made them sound like the little people in that other form of theirs that they showed me in my second dream of them. He told the story in a somewhat scary way, like it was a sinister, frightening experience. "The little green men are bad," he said. "The little people are okay -they're the good ones. But the little green ones are bad. Don't listen to anything they say to you." I felt like they were just messing with him for some reason but what do I know? Again, who knows?)

This oldest guy kind of chuckled and then he asked, "What do you mean? What'd you see?"

The kid said that he and the other boy were just walking around with the flashlight when they decided to walk up to the cook shack (which is kind of off by itself next to the woods at the north-western edge of the grounds) to get a snack. They walked up there and then kind of froze when they saw two little people just chilling there, hanging out by what remained of the cookfire, looking at it, being quiet. "One was sitting on the ground by the fire and the other one was sitting up on the stretcher-" (that year someone had donated an old ambulance stretcher; it doubled as a serving table/dishwashing station) "-hugging his knees. The one on the stretcher jumped off and came over to me."

Here I finally spoke, hungry for details, I suppose. "What'd he look like?"

"He had on a little, uh, breech cloth and his face was painted."

"Like how?"

"It was painted half black and half white with white dots on the black side and black dots on the white side. 'Don't be afraid,' he said, and then he shook my hand."

"How big was his hand?"

"Like the size of a fifty cent piece."

The oldest guy chipped in, "Then what'd he say?"

"He said, 'The reason we show ourselves to you is so that you'll be interested in the Sundance.' After he said that we just took off and ran down here to you guys."

"That's good that you saw them," the oldest guy said. "That's a blessing to see them. Make sure you remember what they told you."

I've always thought that was such a cool experience those boys had because of what that little Indian person told them: "The reason we show ourselves to you is so that you'll be interested in the Sundance." For many, the bulk of what they're looking for inside their spirit, that is responsible for so much of the pain, lostness, grief, anger, dislocation, terrible sadness, innocent poverty of self-knowledge, that they're feeling and dealing with, is to be found in a return to their people, their homelands, their ancient culture and spiritual ways, the things that vibrate with the love and wisdom of their ancestors, the ceremonies, the old songs and stories, the things wet with the lifeblood of prayer, the sweat, the hanblechia, the Sundance. "Heyoka medicine is the most powerful medicine," another Sundance Chief told me, "because sometimes you've got to go backwards before you

can move forward." Many begin to resolve their
internal grief and pains -which are the inherited
parts of their spirit bent grotesquely out of shape
by recent history and the stress of trying to fit into
a radically different culture whose value-system
in practice on both the macro and micro levels is
horribly, insanely far removed from the big universal spiritual heart where it should be, where it was/
is for our Indian people, where it was/has been for
the large majority of Indigenous people and our
species in general- by returning to the things that
saturated our ancestors' lives, by going home, in
a sense, by getting from the ancient culture that
made them a lot of the things this current American
culture seems ill-equipped at best, entirely unable
to at worst, to give them at all. The old culture,
built with prayers and soul from the inside out,
naturally radiates a multifaceted kind of healing
in its very being, like trees or rivers. To be around
it is to be around something that is healing, that
can heal you. The old culture, rich with healing
properties like plants or the human body itself, is
where many Indians will find the things that en-
able them and empower them to answer the gist of
the questions at the beginning of this book, that're
living in the hearts of most Indians around today.
The old culture is a storehouse of wisdom dis-
tilled over ages to readily address these conditions
a spirit and a person can find themselves slowed

down by, hurting with, struggling with, deep in the
spiritual learning with. The old culture pulses with
our ancestors like the cities today pulse with their
electricity. Our ancestors know what it's like to be
completely stuck and engrossed in the mystery of
this human life, and they want to help us because
they have love and compassion for us and their
lives are still connected and entangled with us, as
ours is with them. Our ancestors are the elders of
our elders. They stand wherever the old culture is,
threaded into its spirit. But many, knowing only
the money-and-technology culture of America,
don't know any of this. This is why that little Indian person's statement was so profound.

That little person was giving that Omaha
boy an experience he would never forget so that as
he got older, no matter where his life took him, he
would know in a deep way that the things of his
people were real, that they were not just a bunch
of junk or superstitions or folk tales but that they
were reality, a truer reality than most had any idea
about. That little person spoke of stoking the fire
of the boy's interest in the Sundance because that
interest in an Indian child and even an adult, is like
the branch-tip of the tree of their spirit's nature
poking out into their conscious awareness -break
it off or let it die and it might take awhile to grow
back, as conditions for its doing so are pretty poor
in this day and age; or it might get lost for good,

depriving them of this area of basic intuitive guidance. The boy's interest was a cord he could use to follow his way back to the Sundance and the culture, both of which would be waiting for him with the endless things they had to give him. It is a special blessing to know that the things of the Spirit and the spirit-world are real and exist. This special blessing can and often does make all the difference in a person's life-journey. The little people cared about this young boy. Inside his spirit they saw the story of our Indian people today and they wanted him to be able to find his way back someday, if he ever got lost, if he ever needed to. They gave him a breadcrumb. In a way, they gave a lot of us a breadcrumb.

"Follow the trail of breadcrumbs and you'll be able to find your way back..."

That summer there were maybe about sixty or seventy people there at the Sundance. A couple other boys had a late night encounter with the little people too, also up at the cook shack. "We went up there to get a snack," one of these boys said, "and when we got there it looked like two little kids were digging around in the cookies and crackers. I shined my flashlight at them and yelled, 'Hey! What're you doing?!', and when they turned

around they weren't kids but two of those little
people. When we saw it was them we took off and
ran."

This was a family Sundance. I was the
only person there who wasn't somehow family
or known to the family. It was all Indians, mostly
from Santee and Cheyenne River, except for one
single white kid who'd come along with the kids of
the guy who'd invited me who was from Omaha. I
remember sitting by the sweat during the day when
one of the leaders (a guy who did his first Sundance with Fools Crow when he was a teenager)
talked with this white kid some about the little people. This boy was kind of feeling left out because
so many of the other children were seeing them
and he hadn't.

"They mostly show themselves to the little
kids and remain hidden from the adults. Don't feel
bad. I've been coming here every summer -but
one- for almost thirty years and I've never seen
them, I've never seen those little people."

This leader had a strong gift and would later
take over as Sundance Chief. I thought that was
kind of strange/interesting that in three decades of
dancing at Hidden Valley he'd never seen them.
Hmm, you know?

And then this kid saw them too.

"I was sitting up at the tables by myself
at the cook shack," he said, "just thinking about

stuff, when it was like something hit my hat-" he patted the back of his baseball cap "-from behind me. I looked back and didn't see anything so I just thought it was nothing -but then a few seconds later something else hit my hat again and it bounced off and I saw it was a little twig. This time I turned around and I saw one of those little people peeking around the corner of the cook shack, looking at me and smiling."

This kid, maybe fourteen, looked happy, included. Eager for more details, I asked him, "What'd he look like?"

"He had like a headband with a curtain of feathers hanging over his face but since he was leaning around the corner all the feathers were hanging off the side, away from his face. He smiled at me and I got up to go over to him but then he was just gone and I didn't see him anymore."

The medicine of the little people was strong and scattered all over the Sundance that summer. For those who don't know, this is not the case for Sundances in general, not to my knowledge at least. Every Sundance is a little different for all sorts of reasons; this one was different in its potent addition of the little people to its yearly ceremony; and they were such a part of the mix by simple virtue of the dance's proximity to those woods where the little people have lived for who knows how long. I heard one of the elders say, "I try to come down here every couple weeks to leave something for them, to make them an offering. They help our family and I'm grateful for that."

The third night of purification I again stayed up late by the fire listening to everyone talk and bullshit and share stories. Maybe about three AM or so I was barely keeping my eyes open so I told one of the young guys, one of the singers I was clicking with, that I was going to crash out in the lodge for a bit and to wake me up in an hour or so (my tent was still thirty miles west back at the powwow grounds in Niobrara). He said sure and then I crawled into the lodge, pulled my hoodie up over my head, watched the flames for a minute, felt the magic of the Sundance steaming out of the ground all around me in the darkness, felt like I was made of pure luck for having found my way there, for getting to experience any of it at all, for being alive at all, and then I fell asleep.

Sleeping there in the lodge I had a power-ful, four-part dream. One full dream flashed into another full dream which flashed into another full dream which then flashed into another full dream. This dream contained instructions. The only part I can relate here was the last part. In that part the little people took me to a house of theirs some-where out in the country. We all sat at a picnic table and the head guy of their group of about six or seven talked to me about some things. He gave me two things and then talked to me about some other tribes. At this point I was all about learning as much as I could about all this Indian stuff for my Ponca people, to bring back as much of the lost culture as I could for us, because our tribe is so culturally impoverished and is working with so little compared to other tribes, like our relatives the Lakota. (I was full of big dreams back then. I wanted to bring back the library of our lost Ponca ways, make it available to everyone who was interested, see our people Sundancing again, see us doing our own ceremonies again, getting back our own unique stories, medicines, bundles, sacred knowledge, the language, everything, everything that we used to have.) So after listening to this head guy talk I asked him what was always, always on my mind: "But what about my tribe, what about us Poncas?"

"Don't worry about it," he said, smiling like a grandfather. "We're taking care of it."

I felt reassured. I could also feel the dream ending. And then I woke up.

When I woke up there was just one guy left sitting by the fire by himself, everyone else had finally gone to sleep. I don't think I slept much longer than an hour as it was still dark out but that was all very far away from my mind. I was buzzing from head to toe with the energy of the dream.

It was like the dream was still going on inside
my body and my spirit was still flowering with
a heightened sense of things, like the soul of the
world was completely visible to the enlarged eye
of my feeling -the night shimmered unforgettably
with an extraordinary beauty that swept over me
and everything like a great mythological wind.
Honestly, and this was not a regular thing with me,
I felt kind of high, crisply alert, flush with a high-
grade spiritual happiness. I told the guy by the fire
that I was going to head back to Niobrara, to my
campsite, and take a shower.

I got in my car and, as quietly as I could,
drove out of there, waves of the dream joyful-
ly washing through me, the stars illuminating
all the old land, the stretches of trees, the curves
of the road. I drove back to Niobrara and then a
few miles more to the powwow grounds with my
whole body practically spewing this rare joy all
over the inside of my shitty car, out the window
into the rushing wind and onto the highway. I don't
know how to explain it. I imagine that if I make
it to the end of my life having done everything I
came here to do that I will again feel some portion
of the complete and spiritual happiness and joy
that I felt during that drive. Something about it still
calls to me and I can still feel it.

Showers don't happen every day at the
Sundance and if you're dancing you for sure ar-

en't going to get a shower in for at least four days. It'd been a few days since I'd showered, and that's after working hard all day long in the sun and the hundred degree weather. Finally getting to shower is always its own beautiful high note at the Sundance and this night was no different. I remember smiling and thinking about that dream, pulling into the empty powwow grounds, seeing my lonesome tent by the buffalo pasture, parking by the restrooms/shower building. This was how the ancestors and the little people and the Creator were answering my prayers, taking care of me, helping me to learn things so that I could help my people, how they were responding to my ultimatum. The lightning of the Spirit had struck me and burned me crisp. My whole body smoking like a guy in a cartoon, I smiled with love and took myself a long, hot shower.

After the dance was over I eventually found myself getting to have a conversation with the Sundance Chief. I told him about my dream. "When did you have that dream?" he asked. "A few days ago, during purification." "What do you think it means?" We sat on two fold-out chairs over by his family's tent. I felt like the kid I was back then. "I don't know," I said.

We talked about my dream and then we talked about a piece of the big dream I had when that
little old man came to me and told me his name,
told me to call him and he would come to help me,
and then we talked about the little people.

"They live in the woods over there. A lot
of people think they live inside the trees but they
don't. One time I was at home and they came for
me and they took me to where they live. They have
villages underground and they use the trees as
doorways to go down into them. For awhile they
quit coming around the Sundance here because
they didn't like some of the things they were seeing. But now they've started coming back. The first
year I ran it I saw them come out of the woods and
go from tent to tent blessing and praying for everyone. They had their own little medicine man with
them and he was leading them, shaking his rattles
and praying."

I listened very closely to everything this
man had to say. To some degree, he was what I
was looking for: another spiritual Indian person
whose heart and character resonated with the
depths of mine and who knew about the little people and could tell me about them and validate my
own growing experiences with them. His words
wove ornate pictures in the air that then quickly
phased into different parts of me. If most people
just had a single bag they dug things out of to un-

lock what was being brought up and pondered, he pulled from all sorts of bags, pots, bundles, containers, back packs, car trunks, and underground caches. Even then I recognized the relief I felt at having such a satisfying encounter with some real knowledge that rang trustworthy, that was almost literary in its eloquence, and born of experience. This conversation had under those immense Cottonwoods, finally getting to ask someone about the things I wanted to know about who carried decades worth of hard-earned knowledge about those exact things and more, was not one that joined the river-like blur that would come to contain my own decade-plus worth of conversations with relatives about sacred things -this one would cement itself and remain a clear and important point in my past. In time this man would become my hunka-brother, my adopted brother. We would dance together, cry together, talk in dreams, he would pierce me and tell me of the things he saw when I was trying to break free. The following year he would come to me in a dream and we would talk about me coming to Hidden Valley to Sundance. A few months after that I would be dancing out there with him and his family. That first Sundance, in between rounds while resting, I would have a dream of him and I standing out in front of my old high school in Columbus, the sky full of hundreds of spirits, crowding the air like all those Macy's Day Parade balloon characters had fled in the night and were now converging overhead, looking down at us and giving us their attention. He would call a spirit and it would come from one direction and then I would call another one of the same kind and it would come from another direction. I'd wake up and tell him about it. He'd look somewhere else inside his eyes for a second and then he'd return and say, "You and I are going to be walking together for awhile."

The thing about the little people that he explained and impressed upon me during that conversation though was that they possessed all of the cultural and spiritual knowledge that my Ponca people used to have but seem to be mostly just walking around the vestiges, the ruins, the ghost of today. ("Not many Poncas practice the old ways anymore," he said.) The little people had access to the archives, so to speak, the architectural blueprints to the entire body of all our old ceremonies, our song library, all our old stories, all that was unique to us, all that was once ours. The little people helped our people with all this stuff in the old days and they continued to try to help us even now, despite all the massive static and amnesia of the times. This conversation gave me a bunch of leads and material that would assist me in understanding many things in time but one thing it helped clarify for me was this: these little people were helping to

generate a remembering and a spirituality inside
of me that was kindred to the lost, true stuff of my
ancestors that I was then to share, pass on, hand
out, break off pieces of and distribute for the sake
of helping this same remembering process that
was going on inside of my relatives individually
and my tribe as a whole. It wasn't exactly obvious
to me then at the age of twenty five but it became
so as he explained it to me -the little people were
helping me to grow what used to live in and define
the exalted lives of my ancestors inside myself
so that I could know it from within and get busy
with the work of feeding it into the stream of our
collective, interconnected lives, to help with the
nurturing and sparking of so many of those struggling germs of our ancestral inheritance -the spirit
and medicine and wisdom our ancestors suffered
and sacrificed and broke their backs for that flowed
within our blood and soul. The little people were
continuing on with their traditional relationship
with the Poncas and the Indian people of this land,
a partnership going back to time immemorial, and
my relationship with them was an example of this.
What grew in my life because of their help and
blessings, we all dreamed of seeing regenerated to
its full stature inside all of our people, inside all
people. "When it's present inside a person," my
friend told me, "they say they intuitively know
how to live. They say they live with a reverence

that guides them spontaneously."

I still think regularly, sometimes nightly, about this thread that my hunka-brother clarified for me in regards to the little people and their objectives and myself in that conversation we had that day. For everything that we struggle with and hurt over, there is a journey we can take or a medicine we can learn about to get some healing or find some peace with the struggle or hurt. The questions are like their own answers flipped inside out and if we ask them long enough, stick with them long enough, in time, with experience, they will grow into realistic, empowering understandings that're many times like answers and then some. The problems of the people, the grief and trauma, are working themselves out, crying themselves out, addressing themselves, applying their ancient genius to the whole of what is responsible for all our people's horrific suffering, bit by bit, in the smallness of our own personal lives. One of the main ways, one of the most sacred ways because it is the way of our ancestors, to contribute to this work that is occurring in every corner of our people's soul, is to face it and dig into it as it is densely, complexly, painfully present within our own lives and the lives of our relatives around us. The strings threaded through us all, that unite us all, have been tangled beyond all reason by what has happened in the last couple hundred years; but wherever we untangle it inside ourselves and in the people around us, the whole thing becomes that much more free and energized in untangling everywhere else in all of our relatives. As we learn what it takes to disentangle this shit inside ourselves, we learn what we need to help our relatives with the same frustrating, maddening work of disentangling the shit inside themselves. Doing this work returns our lives to the prayers and thoughts and spiritual ways of our ancestors -it accomplishes that return that we feel a deep yearning for because helping our relatives who are in need, helping the people, has always been at the center of our people's hearts and way of life. We set ourselves upon this road of helping out with these daunting, colossal problems and we find ourselves getting washed over by many of the things that we are looking for in the deeper strata of our soul, we find ourselves beginning to answer and understand many of these basic questions that express the challenges, circumstances, and struggles of our relatives today.

An old man in the sweat: "The purpose of life is helping others."

Crow Dog: "You have to have a heart for the people."

My friend: "We have to learn to sing so that we can teach our children to sing someday."

My friend's grandpa who came to me in a dream: "If I don't do these things, then who will?"

This whole line of thought really opened up for me that day under those Cottonwoods. "Everything that we've lost, they still have," my hunka-brother told me. "Those little people -they are what we should be."

One last little people story from that first summer at Hidden Valley-

That summer, before I went up to Niobrara, I had a handful of dreams that wound up sort of revealing themselves as presentiments of things that happened during my two months of camping out and going to these Sundances and other things. This was all like strange proof of our culture's power and of the semi-mapped out nature of my own destiny (the rest is improvised).

One of the dreams had was this: while napping on my couch in my apartment back in Lincoln I dreamed that I floated up and out of my body. The space I was in was suddenly flush with a swirling, disorienting mass of colored lights that had me twisting and spinning all over the place and it alarmed me and so, circling like a rag doll in the wash, I began to pray and call my helper and call the little people. As I prayed I was, in a flash, teleported somewhere else entirely.

I found myself standing in a stable, new

dream, looking down at this grey ledge of rock that was protruding from a wall of rock in front of me. On the ledge were two somewhat disc-like rocks small enough to be grabbed by a hand. They both had rudimentary faces on them, eyelike indentations, nose divot, screwy mouth line. I felt like they were there for me, sacred stones I was supposed to pick up. I picked up one with each hand and then I turned around to see where I was and what I should do next.

Turning around, I saw that I was in some high-ceilinged underground cavern that went for miles and miles. At a certain point in the distance I couldn't see the cavern's roof anymore, giving it the appearance of almost like having its own weird darkened sky. Also, everywhere, as far as the eye could see, the floor of this cavern was covered in these smallish stones with basic carved faces on them. I knew I was dreaming and knew I should try to remember it. To remember it, I told myself, "I'm in the land of the stone faces," and then I started walking.

I walked along through this cave, stepping around all the stones, looking around, and then the little people appeared back and behind me some. I could feel them and yet, when I looked behind me, they were not visible to me. I kept walking and talked to them. "Could you guys let me see you? Could you make yourselves visible for me? I like seeing you guys. It makes me happy." I told them this, kept walking, but for whatever reason they stayed invisible to me, shadowing me but remaining somewhat hidden.

Then they compelled me to sit down and I did so. I felt their influence come into me and they began to work my arms in this strange ritual motion. Sitting there, they made my fingers touch three times, once at belly-level, once at chest-level, and then once above my head, and then they brought them down back into my lap. I looked at my hands. My fingers looked funny, they were kind of twisted together in two groups like bread ties. "Could you do that again," I asked them, understanding that they were trying to show me something, "so that I can remember it." They repeated the three-part ritual motion with my hands, I thought about what it was all about, and then I woke up.

Skip ahead to about three months later, up at Hidden Valley, after the dance had ended, after I'd talked with my hunka-brother, and a few carloads of us were all swimming down at the Missouri River later that evening. The dancers were all ecstatic, tossing shampoo bottles to each other as they floated off a ways from the shore, laughing, yelling at each other, washing their hair. There was a remnant of an old bridge jutting from a more elevated part of the shore that people were running

and jumping off of. The bluffs across the river
were like pale old books full of stories written in a
lost language. The sky stretched on forever. Down
river white people cruised around in their tiny little
boats.

We all just swam and washed up and
screwed around. The joy of a journey made and
finished together was palpable, something accomplished and added to the mass of life within, something impossible for anyone or anything to ever
take away. I was quietly there in the mix, following
suit, like an adopted kid reunited back with his
welcoming, extended birth family. After maybe a
little over an hour people began to dry off, sit on
cars and smoke. Down by the bridge piece everyone was jumping off there was just the one-lunged
veteran and his boy from Red Lake. During the
Sundance, for whatever reason, as the boy's dad
danced, this kid kind of got in the habit of sitting
by me and following me around when we weren't
all too busy doing other things or when he wasn't
off playing with the other kids. Although quiet
myself, I talked to him and treated him like a little
buddy. His dad noticed this and talked to me quite
a bit, maybe in thanks for looking after his son
some while he was dancing. Maybe drawn by the
warmth of that connection, I ran and jumped off
the bridge piece once last time to join them.

I disappeared down deep into the waters of

the Missouri and then I swam back to where this guy and his son were bobbing in the water by the wall of this bridge piece. The three of us rocking up and down there in the water, I asked them, "So what're you guys doing?" The son piped up, "We're collecting rocks." And then the father said, "We're swimming down to the bottom and then grabbing rocks, looking to see what we find. Like look at this one." He picked one up from their row and held it up to me. "This one has a face on it."

The moment I saw it I recognized it from my dream I'd had a few months back. It was too crazy: this father and son were swimming down maybe fifteen feet to blindly grab rocks off the bottom of the Missouri River and they found one with two eyes, a nose and a screwy smiling mouth, exactly like the one I'd been given in a dream a few months earlier? Uncharacteristically, I spoke up. "I was given a rock with a face on it just like that in a dream a few months ago."

This one-lunged Sundancer handed the rock to me.

"Here then, I guess this is yours."

I took the rock and looked at it closely. This was the way sacred things were supposed to come to a person. Unbelievable. We all three climbed back out of the river and rejoined everyone else, who were getting ready to go. I put my shirt and shoes back on, put the rock in my shorts pocket.

On the drive back to the Sundance grounds I listened to the young guys make their jokes and tease
each other and looked out the window at the mysterious land of our ancestors -overlaid with roads
and telephone poles but still powerfully, utterly
itself.

    One summer early in the morning of our
third day of dancing up at Hidden Valley, I woke
up on my cot and heard my hunka-brother talking
quietly to my main buddy from Omaha who
was on his own cot beside mine under the arbor.
I didn't immediately open my eyes. There was
an intentional quietness to my hunka-brother's
voice, like he didn't want to stir something that
could've been listening. I rolled over and looked
at my Omaha buddy and our Chief crouching
down beside him. It was cold, the sun wasn't up
yet, everyone else but for the fire keeper was still
asleep. Immediately, I heard what our Chief must
have been talking about. Across the creek, in the
woods, clear as day, a drum was being hit, like the
drumbeat we Sundancers knew in our bones and
souls but smaller, perfectly audible, steady, back in
those trees, near and kind of otherworldly. "It's the
chahochina," my brother said.
    Slowly, one by one, the other fourteen or so

dancers flipped off their blankets and sleeping bags underneath the arbor, stretching and blinking, and as soon as they did we quietly pointed out to them the little people's drumming across the creek. We all got up, got ready, used the outhouse, lit up our first cigarettes of the day, walked cold and bare-foot, in nothing but our dirty trunks, over to the fire. We stood there and warmed ourselves, talked and laughed but kept it down, listened to our little relatives hitting their drum, doing their ceremony over there.

It lasted for about twenty minutes and then it faded out, leaving only the silence typical of the early, early morning. We all smiled and read each other's eyes. It was going to be a good day. And it was.

A dream-

I'm where I'm at in real life in this dream: I'm asleep on my army cot in my tent at the Sun-dance. It's night and I'm awoken by the sound of tiny little steps walking across the cheap synthetic material of my tent's floor. One chamber of my spirit fills with the smoke of the happy sweetness that I can feel in their aura; another chamber fills with some good old fashioned natural human nervousness, of the kind that sometimes comes when we're in the presence of non-human entities who're in possession of an intelligence greater than ours. I hear another set of little chahochina feet coming across the floor of my tent, coming over to where I'm at. It's chilly out. One of them hops up onto my cot and then together they use their little hands to kind of pull the flap of my sleeping bag over my face, almost like a pair of mothers tucking me in to protect me from the cold. There's this maternal, caring note to their action, a softness and attentiveness to the way they are looking after me. I keep my eyes closed, keen to the hyper-real nature of what's happening. I am comforted by this dream of my helpers and then I wake up.

That year at the Sundance we all hit a couple pretty big bumps in the road. It was the sort of stuff that I've heard of less-tight Sundances really wilting in the face of. But we, all knowing each other like we did, banded together and overcame, bonded together even closer because of it. My one buddy from Wichita was a little thrown by the unexpected challenges. I let him in on the secret of my dream, which was glowing the whole time in my belly like some extra kind of unwavering strength. "The little people came to me last night," I told him. "This is not the end. It's gonna be okay. We're a strong family. We can handle this shit."

Stocking shelves overnights at the grocery store, listening to my scruffy coworker, a white guy about fifteen years older than me: "When I was at the pen my cell mate was this Omaha guy. He said that one time during their peyote ceremony he decided to leave for whatever reason and that when he opened the flap of the tipi he stopped dead in his tracks because he said there were like a hundred of those little people just standing there in the night looking back at him."

Driving up to Omaha for a sweat with this old friend of mine who's in his late fifties: "When my dad would stay up at Bear Butte he'd leave pieces of rock candy on the fence posts for the little people. He said that sometimes when he'd get up real early in the morning he'd see them coming down from that mountain to come and take that offering of his candy."

Helping the young adolescent son of this one heyoka get things ready to mow at his dad's Sundance grounds: "That year you didn't go up to Joe Bad's Sundance we were in one of his sweats and I saw two of those little people come in there when the door closed. They grabbed Joe's rattles and started running around and flying all over in there, touching everyone."

An old white Vietnam Vet telling us about
his first hanblechia in the lodge: "I kept waking up
and I could feel someone looking at me. I'd open
my eyes slowly and see one of those little people
peeking out from behind my flag, looking at me
and smiling, and then they'd vanish back behind
that flag and I couldn't see them anymore. This
kept happening during the night. I knew it was a
good thing."

Listening to the old man who's pouring
water in the sweat talk about his drinking days as
a younger man: "One time we were all partying
at my cousin's in Omaha and we were up late, we
were all smashed, and then my cousin saw this little person over in the living room. 'Look! Look!,'
he said. We all looked and saw him and then he
went running. We were all drunk so our first in-
stinct was to go and try to catch him. We all started
running after him and he went this way and that
and got away from us. We were knocking all sorts
of stuff over, just crazy, and then he ran down into
the basement and we were like, 'We've got him
now! There's no exit for him down in the basement!' So we all went down there and he was just
standing there, like he was waiting for us, and then
before we could pounce on him and capture him he
just ran right into the wall like it wasn't even there

and vanished. We were always just acting like a bunch of idiots back then and I think that little person was kind of playing with us to point that out."

Sitting by the fire with an old Yankton medicine man: "One year at our Sundance my fire keeper was supposed to wake me up at four thirty so I could do some things and he told me that he had accidentally fallen asleep and almost slept through when he was supposed to wake me up. But he said he luckily woke up right at four thirty because he felt someone tap him on his shoulder in the sweat where he was sleeping. He said he woke up and saw two of those little men smiling at him and running around in the dark like they were at a playground. They woke him up, ran around some and then took off. Then he came and woke me up, just in time."

Talking with this younger Yankton medicine man up at Crow Dog's: "I went down to New Mexico to help some relatives build a new lodge and we got the new one mostly built but my relatives wanted to sweat in their old lodge that night so we did our ceremony in there. Well, during the sweat we began hearing this drumming and singing coming from that new lodge and some of the people in there started getting a little worried, spooked about what was happening over there. They asked

me what was going on and so I asked my helpers
and they told me that the little people were having
a ceremony in our new lodge because whenever
you build a new sweat you're supposed to have a
ceremony in it that night. We didn't do this and I
didn't know this, so those little people were kind of
getting our backs and taking care of it for us. Now
I make sure we always sweat in a lodge the day we
build it. That's how I learned about that."

Talking to my hunka-brother by the fire:
"The one time ------- went to fast we set him up in
the woods, in a spot we have by where those cho-
hochina live. ------ has a gift but he also kind of
tries to deny it to himself and he was barely twenty
then when he decided to fast. I knew something
was going to happen because even as we were
getting him all set up in his altar those little people were already there, standing around with us
and waiting for us to go. We got him set up, sang
and then all came back to over by the sweat fire.
And no shitting, it wasn't ten minutes later, maybe enough time for us all to have a cigarette, and
here came ------- running at full speed right out of
those woods with nothing but his trunks on. He
ran straight into the lodge. 'Are you done?' I asked
him. 'I'm done,' he said. When we went back over
there to get his stuff all of his blankets were neatly
folded up, the offerings in the bowl were gone and

it was on the stack of blankets, and the rest of his stuff was all nicely gathered up too, just waiting for us to carry back to the grounds."

Whenever I'd travel up North for a funeral or powwow or because I was going to visit someone, I'd stop in at Hidden Valley to walk the Sundance grounds, put my hands on and pray at that tree, and leave some offerings by the creek for those little people. I'd pray and sing and feel myself flooded with a closeness to all the things the Sundance was for our people. To remember was to be taken into a holy place. I felt grateful to have experienced so much of the spirit that defined our people, that upheld us, that carried us, that infused us and was the source of us. Those grounds were as sacred a place to me as any other I could've imagined.

One time after I made my offerings and was just walking around there by myself, my mind was suddenly filled with this enormous golden light and I began to really hear those little people talking to me a lot and very clearly. I sat down on a log chunk by the skeleton of the sweat and listened to them talk to me about my life, the Sundance, my Indian people and spiritual things. They talked to me for about fifteen to twenty minutes and then they retreated back into the woods. I was a little shaken by the clarity and length of their communication but I'd experienced enough things by then that I just put it behind me in the library of my experiences with all the rest. I recognized the blessing of it and then continued on with my trip.

A few weeks later I went to visit this old medicine man and this experience came up in the course of our meandering conversation. Sometimes when visiting this particular man his spirits would come into the living room when we were talking -I'd see them or feel them- and our conversation would switch tracks and he'd begin telling me what they were telling him. This time he stood and moved out of his rocking chair and sat in the other chair beside it. "Now this is not what I have to say," he said. "This is them talking. Those little people who were talking to you are your helpers. They used that light you saw in your mind to get your attention so that you'd listen to them, so that you'd be able to catch what they wanted to tell you. You won't see that light next time. Now you know what they sound like so you can recognize when they're talking to you. You are their representative in this world. They will help you and protect you. You have nothing to worry about. Everything will be good."

That medicine man and I talked more that day ("My dad sang for Fools Crow and he told me

the song Fools Crow used to call the little people
into his ceremonies.") about all sorts of things but
it was after that that I began to hear and experience these relatives of mine a lot more explicitly
in my waking life. They came in the sweat when
I called them but then they started coming to me
in the car, at work, at my crappy downtown apartment, at the coffee shop, wherever. Maybe once or
twice a week on average they'd come and tell me
things, just like extremely knowledgeable elders
calling you up to give you some deep understandings about some things quick. One year my hunka-brother told me, "First you feel them, then you
hear them, then you see them." I was in my late
twenties and practicing my spirituality like a beast
for the sake of my people and this was just like
an unexpected but apparently organic part of my
development with the walk of my medicine and
spirituality. There was never a shade or wrinkle of
iffiness to their communications. It was pure spiritual trust of the soundest kind and quality. Everything they told me had the ring of truth, passed the
test in resonating with that most sensitive knowing
deep part in my heart. My stuff was growing and
what I was able to do for my people was increasing
as well. One night in my apartment they told me
this: "There is a big hole in you that we are able
to send a lot of things through to help your people
and loved ones. It's big because of how much you

have sacrificed. The size of this channel in people is determined by their sacrifices. For people who are willing to sacrifice only a little, only a little can come through them. For those who are willing to sacrifice a lot, a lot can come through them to help their people." From these relatives of mine I learned a lot about our people's spirituality and how spirituality worked for human beings in general. "The reason you experience all of these things is so that you can help others who're experiencing all of these things too," they told me. Their wisdom added up and it all kind of made sense. I let it all float to the back of me and begin to grow there. It was all a lot to consider.

Our people have learned from our relatives of the plants and the animals and the other spirits since the beginning. There was a time when it wasn't just human beings and then everything else. There was a time when all relatives talked and communicated, when all understood each other. We as Indian people wished to survive, to thrive, to glow with goodness, to utilize the genius and gifts the Creator had put inside our bodies and souls, to be a working, helping, honoring, sacrificing, praying, singing, dancing organism of intelligent beauty on the earth and in the cosmos. We remembered and listened to the spirits of our ancestors. We shaped our culture around the upbringing of our children, so that when they got older they

could continue our sacred way of life and raise
their children to do the same. The true history of
the world and cosmos turned inside of us with
maximum beauty and poetry. And our spirits were
more fully awake so we were able to converse with
all of these other relatives of ours, stones, animals,
gods, lakes, mountains, star people, little people,
the trees.

Our Indian people lived in this sacred, spiritually awake way for so long that it altered us
genetically and wired us so that our spirits could
maintain a high degree of the remembrance they
enjoyed while discarnate in the pre-birth realms
when they entered into the womb and began to
grow into a body and begin a new human life for
whatever sacred purpose they were called in by
our Mother Earth this time around (to varying
degrees, of course). In short, this amounted to our
Indian people bringing their accumulated spirituality into this life with them and getting a body that
was genetically primed through our people's way
of life to support the kind of active spiritual day-
to-day existence that now seems made up or like
sheer mythology to the predominantly spiritually
asleep people of today's modern world. In talking
about this with a friend, he said, "They say that in
the previous Age every step we took was a prayer.
What you're talking about is what they were re-
ferring to. We were practically a different kind of

being back then. What we are today is basically a developmentally retarded version of our ancestors."

One summer I was talking to my uncle and he said, "Indians are naturally spiritual." We are still living off the thousands upon thousands upon thousands of years that our relatives lived in life-benefiting, future-generations equipping and blessing harmony with our Mother Earth, the rest of Creation, and the Great Spirit. These relatives we share our blood with -radiant with humanity- are still echoing through us in countless, manifold ways, and this natural spiritualness is an essential, undying part of this. We Indian people still naturally and spontaneously experience a lot of things these great and robust ancestors of ours experienced. We have some of their abilities, their knowledge, their ingrained instincts for helping the people, loving the land, loving our non-human relatives, for devoting ourselves to the sacred, to the love-natured mystery of the Spirit. (This includes reaching out to help everyone in the hoop, including non-Indians, whom we're now mixed into on all sorts of levels, blood and spirit and everything else.) Dreaming of, experiencing and working with our spirit-relatives is a small part of this.

My hunka-brother told me, "I've been seeing the spirits since I was a little guy stumbling around in my Pampers." My friend, in speaking of

his grandpa, said, "Because of his walk of life he
had one main helper and this helper was always
with him, whether he was flying somewhere on
a plane or whatever -his helper was always with
him." In every Indian community there are some of
our people who still are spiritually awake enough
to relate to the spirits in the way that our ancestors
did. We still have Indian doctors, people whose
primary calling in life is to work with the spirits
to help the people with all sorts of matters. Others
have different roads to walk but still have enough
of their ancestors' ability to know the spirits some,
to understand that Other World some, to have a
relationship with the specific spirits that are like
their family members in that Other World. These
specific spirits, whether they be ones who work
with an Indian doctor or with a regular individual,
are generally referred to as a person's spirit-helpers
or spirit-friends. So these little people have been
my helpers, my friends. They have helped me with
my spiritual life, my daily life, in ceremony, with
just all sorts of little things here and there. They
have helped my loved ones, my friends, people
I've only crossed paths with once or only knew
for a short period of time. They gave me the idea
to write this book, have even talked to me about it
some when I've set my writing stuff down to go
and use the restroom. One time I asked a friend,
"How come these spirits keep coming to us even

after we fuck up so much or are just uncool ass-
holes?" He thought about it for a second and then
he said, "Because they have a lot of hope for us."
In the old days our relatives worked with their
helpers to ensure and tend to the health and happiness and survival of the people -nowadays, even
with everything being so radically different, that
work remains the same.

For the past nine years I've worked overnights as a clerk at a gas station here in downtown
Lincoln. I work by myself, have no coworkers, no
boss breathing down my neck. I read, write po-
ems, listen to crazy late-night AM radio, meditate,
space out, think, and bullshit with my customers
all night. There's a lot of quiet at my job and the
little people have come to me many, many times
while I've been there, when I'm mopping, washing something in the back sink or meditating in
one of our booths. They tell me things and I listen.
Sometimes they come strong and I feel their sacred
power like a sudden moment of tearful feeling;
other times their understandings just come real fast
into my head, like a quick telepathic download.
This is what it's like to be humbly half woven into
the world of the spirits. This is what it's like to be
able to hear your helpers.

For awhile before I quit smoking they'd
come a lot of times when I'd step outside for a cigarette. I'd look at the crescent of moon and brush
of stars and relax back into the moment with the
smoke. They'd show up and we'd begin talking or
I'd just listen. One time they told me something
interesting about tobacco, about why it's sacred.
They said tobacco has a component in its being
that naturally enhances and clarifies communication between this world and the Other World.
They showed me a long corridor with myself at
one end and the spirits at the other end. We were
trying to talk to each other across this semi-long
distance but the spirits sounded faint to me. Then
they showed me offering tobacco, using it, and
it was like it amplified the sound waves of their
speech, enlarged them, and then I could hear them
better, as if they were standing just a few feet away
instead of down the corridor. Tobacco was sacred
and considered as such by both sides because it
literally improved the quality of communication
between both worlds but also because it represented the value of valuing the communications and
relations between the worlds. Every time a person
offered tobacco they were acknowledging the im-
portance of remembering our relatives in the Other
World and of maintaining relationships with those
relatives. Our Indian people did this regularly
because they understood the necessity of remem-

bering and integrating the reality of this larger,
encompassing spirit-world into their lives and culture. The use of tobacco and its teaching kept this
basic operational understanding of the larger reality close and in the core of people's lives. This was
why tobacco was sacred, they told me. This was
why it was used for offerings among our Indian
people. This was what was inside it.

I have a Lakota friend who used to live
down in Kansas. He teaches the language, is kind
of my main collaborator, my spirit-brother. One
time heading down there, drifting around in my
head on the long drive, the little people suddenly came into my car. The feeling of them had me
half-warhooping for a second like the old-timers
I'd heard making their sounds in ceremony when
the spirits came in. They began talking to me about
my brother and me. They said that he had a gift
and that I had a gift and that when the two of us
were physically together, like in the same place,
our gifts, like two unique substances, combined together to create a third thing, like a third substance,
and that they utilized that special third substance
to do things for the both of us that they maybe
couldn't do as easily or as frequently for us when
we were apart. When they told me all of this they

showed me like a power-point illustration of it all
in my mind. They told me some more stuff too and
then they left and it was back to just me cruising
down the highway, small towns, verdant fields, the
sweet endless blue sky.

One time my brother and I were having a
cigarette and talking about spiritual things late at
night outside his apartment after his wife and kids
had gone to sleep. Somewhat abruptly, he stopped,
and said, "Let's go inside." We went inside and
then he said, "I forgot my cell phone out in the
car. I'm gonna run and get it quick." When he left
I sat down on the couch, closed my eyes, dipped
my head and began praying. Unexpectedly, those
little people came and began telling me some
things. When my brother came in I looked up and
said, "When you were getting your phone I was
praying." He said, "I was praying too." We both
laughed.

"When you were out there the spirits came."

"Huh," he said, unfolding things with his
spirit the way he does, reflecting, silently feeling
his way through to the pith.

"Do you want to know what they said?"

This was all kind of new business to me,
relaying some of what the spirits told me.

"Yeah."

"They said they were out there listening
to us and that they were happy because we were

helping them with their work just by talking about the things that we were." My brother listened as I continued to tell him some more and then we put on the horror movie that we'd rented and kicked back and watched that.

Just to be alive is a sacred thing. Every one of us is a sacred mountain of stories, something worth humbling ourselves before, growing soul, artistic and lyrical in form, housing the Great Spirit, a hoop vibrating with untold generations of life, piercing the heavens, planted in the earth, unique, eternal, mortal, bittersweet, and strange. But we all have some stories that we maybe love to tell a little more than the others, if the conditions are right, because they mean so much to us, or contain something so special and personal to us. Maybe these stories are like the taller trees on our mountain. Somewhere we are all hiking up through the wintry brush with a close friend to go and show them one of these trees, so that they can see one of the things that really embodies who we understand ourselves to be, so that they can join us in experiencing the love and soul that lives in that tree, in that story.

Here's one of mine-

One year I finally got to introduce my brother Clark, my hometown artist big-brother hero mentor kindred-spirit friend, to this Lakota spirit-brother of mine. They'd both been hearing about

each other through me for years and years. They
were like my two best friends. One my white artist
friend and the other my spiritual Indian friend. For
a long time my life had been these two tangled up
halves both trying to continue on with their dreams
and their work -the artist side of me and this spiritual side of me- and these two brothers of mine
were like these two halves of me; and their finally
getting to meet after all these years felt like a sym-
bolic recognition of how these two halves of me
were now sort of together as one inside of me instead of connected but maybe not knowing how or
why; I felt like their meeting signified a serious degree of unity I'd achieved within myself, of understanding how my art and my spirituality were kind
of the same thing in a way, of how I'd matured into
a whole and was no longer so puzzled and un-
clear about my own complicated nature. Clark had
been my art brother since I was a teenager and my
Lakota brother had helped me endlessly as I Sun-
danced and dreamed and experienced all manner of
things while winging it through the tough territory
of the Red Road. And now these two brothers of
mine were finally going to meet. Now, and for the
only time in this life so far, we were all going to be
together.

Clark and I drove the three and a half hours
down to Kansas and then we unloaded our happy,
weary asses from my junker car and moseyed on

down the walk to my Lakota brother's apartment.
We knocked and were welcomed in, were given
coffee, a spot on the couch, greetings from the wife
and kids, waves of warmth that were like a thick
buffalo robe placed over our shoulders, pulling us
down into the goodness of the visit. After about
a half hour my Lakota brother said, "You guys
wanna have a smoke?" Clark and I looked at each
other and then we both started getting up.

The three of us went outside onto the lawn
of my brother's apartment complex. It was beginning to cool down, to get dark. Almost as though
someone had put in a request for it, a massive cin-
ematic thunderstorm was crawling over the tops of
buildings in the distance on the edge of town. My
brother rolled himself a cigarette while Clark got
to work rolling himself and I two fat, perfect ones
(when Clark lived in Lincoln he was always rolling
me these serious not-fucking-around cigarettes to
smoke with him down in his dingy, voodoo-shop
basement apartment). I could feel the specialness
of what was happening, like two legends meeting,
two giants, two geniuses. Without these two brothers I never would've made it, I wouldn't be here to
write these words. These two brothers have helped
me more than anyone else. A memory was being
made that would travel with me for the rest of my
life.

We smoked and filled the air with our laid-back conversation, sitting Indian-style in the grass like a couple of old Indians from those black-and-white photographs from back in the day. Clark sat in the north, I sat in the west, and then my brother sat in the south. They talked and I listened more and smoked, feeling the two of my brothers coming together, enfolded in gratitude, shitty-grinning. Then something unexpected and cool happened. Sitting there, I felt this energy come out of my stomach and move into the space on either side of me, the space between Clark and me and then me and my brother. Then two little people appeared in that energy, in those spaces. I looked at them, kept smoking and listening to my brothers talk. This was a spiritual blessing. My relatives the little people were honoring this special meeting, this special moment; they were adding to the significance of it, underlining it even; layering in their spirit and presence. There were now five of us sitting in a half circle with that monstrous rumbling thunderstorm growing closer at our backs. Clark, a little person, me, another little person, and then my Lakota brother. The little person to my right said, "This is how we talk to the medicine men when they're talking to the people." I mentally nodded to this, what he said, and then I kept on with my brothers. Before we finished our smokes those little people left. Soon after we went inside the storm hit, pounding on the rooftop for hours.

Blessings to the little people who sat with us on that evening years ago. "Inside that tree," I say, pointing, feeling the beginning of something like tears, "the five of us are smoking and the love that binds us all together is shining bright, no, brighter, brighter than anything else in the whole of Creation."

After I had my vision when I was eighteen something came and taught me how to meditate. I learned to silence my mind at will and then rest comfortably, in a relaxed way, inside of that silence. Through that inner silence the Spirit became visible to me and my meditation practice basically consisted of resting in oneness and communion with the perceived and experienced Divine Creator. This practice, perception, and communion has been the root and source of my spirituality ever since.

I usually meditate at home in my recliner. I close my eyes, enter into the silence, rest there and then relax into the oneness that appears when the Spirit is seen. One afternoon I was doing this when I began to feel this anger like clumping up and crapping out of my gut. More of it amassed and then the little people came.

"Why are you so angry?" they asked.

I went into the anger and tried to feel the truth of what it was all about. I saw the little kid of myself angry because of instead of having parents that scooped me up and loved me and protected me, I had parents I had to retreat away from and find a way to survive. I felt abandoned and told those little people so.

"I feel angry because it's like I was abandoned, left to fend for myself as a kid in hellish circumstances. It's not fucking fair."

Then I looked into the anger more and saw myself being bombarded by all the visions and experiences I had when I was a teenager, left alone to wander and cope like a crazy man for years and years with this never-ending stream of spiritual experiences.

"And then I was abandoned all over again," I told them, "when I was given my vision and I had to just handle it all by myself. It makes me fucking angry that I had to just do all this shit by myself."

I kept meditating and felt the long tendrils of that old, familiar, complicated anger unspooling out of me.

"But you didn't have to handle it all by yourself," they said. "We sent you all sorts of teachers to help you along your way."

Still angry, the open blackness of my inner vision was suddenly filled with the images of many of the friends and elders and spiritual people I've

known over the years. I saw Clark, Joe Bad, the
Lakota woman who did that divination, the old
man I'd helped with the sweat for ten years, my
hunka-brother, my other hometown artist mentor
Scott, my Lakota brother down in Kansas. One at
a time I saw an image of these people and when
I did I also instantly saw the one major thing I'd
learned from each and every one of them, and how
that thing then became a core part of my character and way and understanding. They were all like
segments in a circle of relatives who came together
over time to pass on/activate some essential understanding inside my own slowly remembering spirit.
It was undeniably humbling to have these friends
of mine contextualized in this way for me by the
spirits. But I still felt angry.

"But you never sent me a teacher who could
help me with my specific gift, who knows what it's
like to live with what I live with."

"That's because you came into this world
with enough understanding to be your own teacher when it comes to this gift of yours; you have
enough understanding to be your own coach when
it comes to helping this gift of yours emerge from
you and mature."

Their understanding planted itself in the
layers of my spirit behind all the rough, twisting
anger. I've never doubted anything these relatives
have told me (never had a reason to) and I didn't

doubt this. They left and I continued meditating. The answers we get are not always the answers we want. The anger dissipated and I felt grateful for my teachers I had had, that a nobody kid like me in the middle-of-nowhere Nebraska could still be blessed with the knowing of some pretty fantastic spiritual people. I was both comforted and not but also more comforted than not. The song of life in this world resounded beautifully all around me and full of that special quiet, I did my best to listen to it.

The Lakota woman who did that divination for me said, "The little people are community-builders. They want to bring people together, to build up community."

A young leader at our Sundance said, "Those little people used to do rituals in Grandpa Earl's basement. Upstairs everybody would be doing their thing, eating, visiting, whatever, while downstairs you could hear those little people busy doing their rituals, whatever those were."

One day I was sitting in the downtown public library reading Indian Country Today when they showed up and started talking to me. I was reading this article about a pair of tiny old children's handcuffs that were used during the boarding school days. Apparently someone had found them among the boxes left behind by a deceased relative. This person knew what they were and knew enough about the horrors of the boarding schools to not want to just keep them but to maybe do something with them that was in acknowledgement of what had happened, to do something right with them. Residing in the Kansas area, they gave the handcuffs to Haskell Indian Nations University, one time site of the tragic boarding school experience, now an accredited four-year college host to Native students from all across America. Also, at the time, the place where my Lakota brother taught the language.

When I was reading this article the little people came and began to tell me of a ceremony we could do with the handcuffs to help the people, specifically to help heal the continent of pain spanning our people's collective soul that is a result of everything that went down in the boarding schools. I had been told that the little people were ritual-makers, that they were naturally gifted in this area of creation and craftsmanship; now I listened as they described an annual ritual we could do with the handcuffs and the mechanics of how we could do it and what would happen if we did.

They showed me a tree on the Haskell campus grounds. They said that during a selected day every year we could have a ceremony of prayer and remembrance for all the people whose lives were affected and impacted by the boarding schools, both those no longer among us and those still with us. Offerings would be done, songs would be sung, stories would be told, tears would be cried, prayers would be made. The physical centerpiece of the ceremony would be those handcuffs. They said those handcuffs were a concretion of and link to the mass of pain and suffering generated by the boarding school trauma and horrors as it still pervaded our people both in this world and the Other World. They said that we could use those handcuffs as a point of access to that pain continent, pouring our gathered prayers and ritually produced and focused healing energy onto it and into it. They said this healing would flow out to every person who carried a piece of that continent, embodied and ghost, slowly working to wear it down and transform it, to erode it and change it. They said that the healing could flow backwards and forwards in time, unlimited in its reach. They said that just as we could change the story and the use of the handcuffs in our ritual -from prisoner device for young Indian children to ceremonial healing object for Indian people traumatized by the boarding school experience- so too could we change the story of this chapter in our people's history from something that severely wounded us to something we'd healed up from, recovered from, bounced

back from, survived, metabolized in our soul and
were not broken from or ended by. Our people's
genius and resilience could have the final word on
the matter. We would not be defined by and under
the thumb of what happened to us but rather we
would redefine it on our own terms, drawing from
the cultural roots that were at our core, turning the
thing that tried to kill us into a food for the regen-
eration of the very cultural and spiritual things that
made us who we were and gave us life. This was
how they outlined the ritual and its healing to me
telepathically as I sat in the library with the maga-
zine open in my lap.

    Maybe kind of the sad part about this story
is that I of course didn't act on the information that
these helpers of mine gave me. I was a socially
awkward poor loser college drop-out half-breed
nobody who kind of felt like shit on a lot of days.
Who was I to tell anyone anything? I thought about
driving down to Haskell, asking around to find out
who I should talk to (my friend taught there but
even in my fantasy I didn't think about embarrass-
ing him with my lameness), and then telling that
person or those people about what the spirits told
me about this annual ceremony we could do with
those handcuffs to help with the healing of our
people. And then I never thought about it again because I knew that I would never do it. I didn't have
it in me to go and do stuff like that on behalf of

the wisdom of the spirits. I was a nobody and I'd never stand up and go and do anything like that. I ended up writing a poem about what they told me, emailed it to my friend, and that was that.

The other day I was thinking about how the government's campaign of genocide against our people has saturated us so thoroughly, all the way down to the basic conditions of the thoughts we have about ourselves going on in the front of our skulls day in and day out. Their policies communicated the perceived worthlessness of our Indian people, of our Indianness and everything that made us Indian, in their every program and approach, with the boarding schools being a prime example. We were told that being Indian made us inherently worthless and this message began to echo everywhere, in our communities, in our own heads, and especially, infuriatingly, from our mouths as we talked to not only each other but to our children, to our most precious little babies -the government's message of our Indian people's worthlessness became the story we told ourselves about ourselves, the story we told each other, the story we placed and deposited into our children (my friend: "When they took our language away they took away the voice and mind that had evolved alongside and to be in beautiful service to the consciousness and soul that the land and gods had lovingly and with great care grown in our people over untold thousands of years.").

Nowadays all of us Indian people have this layer of worthlessness present inside of us to some degree, oftentimes to a tragically life-ruining degree. The spirits and the ancestors give us dreams and knowledge to help our people and we are too sad or broken or beaten-down to act on it, to do anything with it. The genius of our people struggles and suffers under the mountain of shit heaped upon it by the government's campaign of genocide. But maybe our greatest strength is that we are made from the inside out of stuff stronger than anything that could ever be thrown at us. We have survived for ages. The poem of our life is intimately interwoven with the poem of the life of the land itself. We were dreamed into being by the land and are carriers of and extensions of its own internal spiritual wisdom and love and needs and know-how. As long as the land is here and around we'll be here and around. And this reality is the counter-programming that is slowly but surely echoing back to our people, coming up inside of us through our genius and dreams, our visions and deep personal inner knowing. My worthlessness stopped me from following up on the little people's knowledge and help but the deeper Indian genius active within me due to my ancestors' love and prayers and sacrifices has me writing out these words. One will dissipate when I pass on; the other is made of such stuff that it will carry on, that it will survive, that it will LIVE. You tell me who you think is going to win this one. The thing I didn't do or these words. The genocide-attempt or our people. You tell me who you think will get the final say, which will outlast the other, whose song will be heard in the prairie wind a long, long time from now. You tell me.

Ever since I was a teenager I've gone up to the Ponca powwow with my goofy brother Dan. I've known Dan since I was five years old. My dad and his dad were best friends growing up so to me he's always been my other brother.

When I got into the sweats and my people's culture, Dan, a bearish manchild white truck driver, happily tagged along right in there with me. The spirits started coming to him in dreams, started visiting him in the sweats too. He's the only one of my friends the little people have come to and visited in his dreams over the years. One year before we went up to the powwow he told me this dream: "You and I were walking up the buffalo pasture collecting sage when one of those little people appeared. He was behind you but you didn't know he was there. Something about him made me start laughing and then he grabbed the back of your boxer shorts and gave you a huge wedgie! It was just the funniest thing in the world. I really busted out laughing and then I woke up. What do you think it means?"

"If it made you laugh like that," I said, "then fuck, it just means we're going to have a good time at the powwow this year."

Dan and I always stop off at the Sundance grounds on our way to the powwow as a part of our routine. We leave offerings for the little people, walk around, honor the place just by checking it out and talking, by putting our hands on the arbor, gazing up at the tree, sitting down by the ashes of the sweat fire. A few summers back we did our thing and then continued on the rest of the way to the powwow. When we got there it was all in full swing, friends we hadn't seen in a year were all over. We set up our tent in our family's usual place and then when we were about to get going over to the arbor, Dan got worried, went back to his truck and then confessed something: "I think I lost my wallet back at the Sundance grounds."

My poor buddy Dan was always doing shit like this. One time when we were teenagers I went over to his place to pick him up to take him to the auto parts store. When I got there he was underneath his car on the cement working on it. I sat on the curb and bullshitted with him. After a couple minutes he pulled himself out from under his car

and without saying a word, punched out his headlight. "What the fuck did you do that for?!" I asked
him. "Now we gotta get the part you need AND a
new headlight!"

"I got frustrated," he said, sliding the rest of
the way out.

I shook my head.

"We just got here and now we're gonna
have to drive thirty minutes back there, spend who
knows how long searching for your wallet, and
then drive thirty minutes back? This is going to be
like an hour and a half mission at least. Fuck."

We loaded back up into his beat-up fishing
truck and drove back to the Sundance grounds.

The Sundance grounds are left unused and
unmown for most of the year besides the Sundance and Memorial Day weekend when we put
people up on the hill. So the waist high grass did
us no favors. We walked all over, the sweat, the
cook shack, the arbor, everywhere. It was a lost
cause. He had no clue where it might've fallen out
or where he might've somehow dropped it. It was
a fat overstuffed numskull's wallet. I had no idea
where to look for it. Eventually I went back to the
truck and Dan just kept randomly walking around,
his eyes scanning and trained on the ground.

In the truck I smoked and then I got an idea.
Dan's wallet had all his money in it for the trip,
it had everything he needed. I took some tobac-

co and began praying to those little people in the woods, telling them what had happened and asking them humbly if they could somehow help my brother find his wallet. I prayed and then I dropped the tobacco out the window onto the ground and then instantly I saw this image of Dan's trousers collapsing around his ankles accordion-like in the outhouse, his wallet pooping out of his back pocket in the process. I yelled out the window to Dan, "Check the outhouse! Did you check the outhouse?!" Dan went to the outhouse, vanished for a second and then re-emerged with his wallet in hand. "Got it!"

Bumping along back across the farmer's road away from the grounds, like the asshole only two old friends can warmly be to each other, I said, "Do you know how I knew your damn wallet was in the outhouse? I offered some tobacco and the little people told me. You better thank them because otherwise you'd be fucked."

I almost never called the little people outside of the sweat lodge. Sometimes I'd experience stuff when they came, sometimes I wouldn't and on good faith would just assume they were there. Sometimes I'd feel them come in, sometimes I'd see flashes of things in my head, sometimes they'd

tell me things, sometimes they'd fill my body up
with different powers, like filling up a glass with
different colored waters. They were just a part
of what I experienced when I humbly crawled in
there on my hands and knees to sing and pray with
my relatives.

   One time I had a very close friend who
had been in a bad way for a long time; he was
low, drinking all the time, losing his will to live,
talking suicidal. My friend's pain pained me and I
didn't know what to do. When I went to the sweat
I called those little people and told them what was
up, told them that I didn't know what was at the
root of these chronic inner struggles he was always
breaking down under but that maybe they could
see into it and help him with it somehow, help this
friend who had saved my own ass too many times
to count. After a minute they began talking to me.
"This thing inside of him we cannot take out," they
said. "Only Tunkasila (the Creator) can take it out
of him. Only he can remove it from him." Then
in my inner vision they showed me a white cross.
They said, "This thing is the cross he bears in this
life." The white cross multiplied into a line of
crosses, connected end to end like a string of paper
dolls. "And this is the cross you bear..."

   They told me, without getting into specifics,
that the sacrifices I made in my life, that I made
willingly for my people, generated a substance that

both they and my own spirit used to do the medicine things and the spiritual things I did to help my
people. They said that these things I went without of in my life, and suffered the pains of going
without them, these regularly made and willingly
suffered sacrifices, were the cross that I bore in this
life. They said my friend was in a similar situation;
his spirit had agreed to those long-running suffer-
ings as part of the life and dynamic of his soul's
work. Willing endurance of pain and difficulties
for the sake of life and the people generated a special substance that enabled the deeper powers of
the soul and Creation to do powerful, miraculous
things. The crosses we all bear are the small, personal versions of how we do our part in this work,
in this universal grace and spirituality that we are
all a part of. It's probably more complicated but
that day they told me it was something like that.

So we continue on and carry our cross, hurting under the weight of it, our flesh rubbed raw,
but doing it for all and everything and everyone
that we love.

I'm going to let this little people poem/
praise/storytelling memoir begin to come to an end
with one of the ends from my own life. An end I
didn't see coming. An end that changed me profoundly, that turned into its own new beginning.

When I was about thirty I started having the
first real recurring dream of my life; I'd always

been sort of a prolific dreamer but I'd never really
had a classic recurring dream. My recurring dream
was this: I was traveling somewhere by car with
a close friend or friends and the car would break
down, we'd get out, my friend would help me, and
then I'd wake up. Different cars, different friends,
different locales, but always the same dream story
line. I must've had that dream ten times and then
one night at a sweat up in Omaha the little people
came into the lodge and interpreted it for me.

They said that car represented how I was living my life, the vehicle, so to speak, I was using to
make my way through the journey of my life and
days. They said a change was coming and that the
breaking down of the car meant that I was going
to change how I was living, my priorities and path
and lifestyle, and that I was going to have to find
a new car, a new way, to accommodate the changes I was going to go through. They told me more,
comforting me and reassuring me, but that was the
gist of what they said was going on with these recurring dreams. The changes were appearing in my
dreamlife; soon they would appear in my real life.

It all became clear to me some months later
after my brother Clark moved away to Seattle and
I had a long, no-holds-barred conversation about
life and spiritual things with my other hometown
art friend, Scott, at the coffee shop. After I had
that conversation the strangest feeling began to

grow in my body, unfamiliar and indecipherable. It
followed me, filling me and then receding into the
background of my consciousness, for days. Then
one night at work when there were no customers I
hopped up on the back counter and decided to look
into this strange, body-sized feeling and see what
the hell it was.

I closed my eyes and peered into the feeling
with my spirit and instantly saw and understood
this: I saw the scene from Forrest Gump where
after his mom dies, grief-stricken, he begins running back and forth near-mutely from ocean to
ocean, gathering running companions, becoming
a celebrity, growing a beard, and then one day, on
a piece of highway nowhere in particular, he just
stops. This scene was the scene I saw. Everyone
waits to hear what he's going to say, recognizing
his journey has come to an end. They look at him
wide-eyed and then he says, "I think I'm gonna go
home now." And then he just starts walking home.

I saw this and massively, incontrovertibly,
understood that my journey, my all-in Sundancing-
till-the-day-I-die journey, was done and over too. I
thought I was on a forever ascending journey that
would consume me my whole life until I was an
old man and ready to cross over. I wanted to help
my people with all that I had, with all that I was.
And now I saw clear as day in this big strange
feeling that all that was not all lifelong, at least not

in the way I then understood it to be, but that it was a chapter, a chapter now wrapping up to make way for a whole different chapter. Just as Forrest Gump's grief was working itself out in the odyssey of his years-long coast-to-coast run and then it just suddenly finished itself one day on some random stretch of road, so too was this heroic quest of my own to recover all that was culturally and spiritually lost to my struggling Ponca people a result of something tremendous and deep working itself out in my spirit and now I suddenly understood that whatever it was doing was done and that now that endless spiritual coast-to-coast endurance prayer run search fast recovery-mission of mine was over and that it was time for me to go home, to descend from the mountain of holy hardships and learning and return back to my village, the city, to ordinary life.

    The team that had inhabited the land of my consciousness ever since I had my vision when I was eighteen, who kept the fire of my spiritual questing burning brightly day and night, busy as fuck, endlessly hungry, driven like gods remaking the world, all broke camp and packed up their gear and practically left that night, as soon as I understood what was going on. "We were all completed circles mentoring you and now you're a completed circle. The work is done. We won't see each other as much but we'll still see each other. Now you need to go back home, go back home and be a humble completed circle among your people, with your people, for your people."

From there a new story began. It was like leaving space and coming back to earth, leaving the front lines and returning back to the old neighborhood. It was tough, unexpected. I'm now thirty four and only now barely beginning to figure out what I'm doing, what I'm supposed to do now.

When Joe Bad died, seven years ago today, we had a sweat for him. While loading my pipe I saw his ghost in there. The old man running the ceremony, also loading his pipe, abruptly said, "Joe's here. He's here with us now."

In that sweat the little people came in strong and told me some things. They told me the purpose of what my writing's for, of how it's supposed to help not only our Indian people but whoever reads it. I listened and finally understood how my art and my spirituality were really one and the same thing.

I hope you get out of these words and stories what the little people told me you would in that sweat we had for Joe Bad seven years ago this week.

I hope the things the spirits have told me come true.

I hope they do.

"We need to fix the memory of souls."

"We need to fix the memory of souls...to heal the people."

"Yes, to heal the people."

Deep within all of our souls there is a memory that runs much, much deeper than what has accumulated in the limited span of our current lives. This memory is full of countless compartments of knowing, of an accrued remembering of how to be and how to do a whole host of essential things. Inside this memory of our souls we intuitively remember how to be in rich, fruitful, respectful and sound relationship with all the things and forces and spirits and people we are already automatically in relationship to just by virtue of being alive. The understanding of a great elder is already fully-formed and inside of us all from the beginning. The tree of our soul is dense with rings from breath one. The work is remembering. The work is reconnecting to everything we already know.

This is the memory of our soul.

I spent a lot of time trying to figure out what this meant when I was told it in that first dream I had of the little people all that long time ago, and then it kind of grew into an assignment; like what did he mean and then how exactly to go about fixing it? I chewed and chewed on this and then I think I began to understand it some.

As Indian people we have a particular layer
of our ancestors' memory in our soul and when
that is flowing outwards from within into our
minds and hearts and lives, a certain broad harmony results, a certain inner potential is realized,
something ancient begins to rest openly in us, our
way of being begins to take on the shape of and
resonate with many of the core particulars and val-
ues of our ancestors. When this ancestral memory
of our souls is present we can be humble, mature,
robust, capable, big-hearted, self-sacrificing and
decent Indians and people as our ancestors were.
This ancestral layer of memory is a major piece of
our ancestors' legacy and gift to us. Before the dis-
ruptions and tragedies of the recent era this layer
naturally, organically blessed and crafted our people to a defining extent from the bottom levels up.
This was a seed in the soul of every Indian person
that grew into its intended fruit-bearing tree. But
now, because of everything that's happened, this
seed is buried, dormant, and that memory layer is
something cut off from the majority of our Indian
people, broken in effect, and that's why it needs
fixing. The degree to which it is fixed is the degree
to which their ancestors' magnificence and beauty
is returned to them. When fixed their ancestors'
wisdom will flow in them again.

So how to accomplish this?

This book tells some of how it was some-

what accomplished in me but my answer nowadays is whatever works, works. The Sundance,
powwows, learning the language, spending significant time with old people, helping and serving
the people, going to sweats, singing Indian songs,
making art, gardening, going on crazy, fucked-
up journeys, getting guidance from your dreams,
meditating, prayer, researching, anything, everything, whatever. Try, search, hunger, have faith, do
the work, learn from the others who're on the same
road, who're trying to fix that memory of their soul
so that they can understand themselves. There is
no simple recipe or solution or path; you just gotta
keep doing it until it gets done, bit by bit, little by
little, day by day. If anything maybe this little book
can be a starting point of possible leads for some, a
sheaf of notes or something for others. Follow the
stories and you will get there. Follow your dreams
and you will get there. Follow the remembering
and you will get there.

Whatever works, works.

As the years went on I realized how much
this work did not just apply to the situation of my
Indian people but to so many all over America
and the world. In this day and age we have almost
all been disconnected and enculturated to be insanely and sorrowfully distant from the knowing,
beauty-filled memory of our soul and so in a sense
almost everyone is walking around deeply broken

and in need of this specific kind of fixing. This brokenness, this disconnection from the earth and the Spirit, this lostness, is reflected in our lives and the bankrupt cultures we're living in. This work of remembering is something that desperately needs addressing all over America and a lot of the rest of the world as well. Healing, justice, decency, meeting the basic material and spiritual needs of people everywhere, human rights, peace, purpose, happiness, systemic problem-solving -all of this and more is directly connected to the presence and/ or absence of this remembering in individuals and in communities and cultures. And so in this sense this work is a matter of urgency for all. We need to get all of our connections with this memory of our souls back up and running not only for the sake and quality of our own lives but for the sake and quality of all our loved one's lives, everyone and everything's lives, the life of our precious Mother Earth. We have the knowledge and spiritual crafti-ness within ourselves; we just have to remember it.

We walk this road together, relatives.

Let's see how great our remembering can become.

Mitakuye Oyasin.

Lincoln, Nebraska
November 2015

ACKNOWLEDGEMENTS

Mountains of gratitude to Jacques Le Breton for
the beautiful, killer cover, to Kim Wayman for
tenderly handling all the pages between, and to
Amanda Huckins for crafting this book in its
original incarnation, all 285 hand-folded copies.

Made in United States
Troutdale, OR
05/13/2024

19827158R00072